In Memory of

Roger E. Allen

Presented by His Loving
Wife & Children

Mary Allen

Brad Allen

Nancy Talarico

Betsy Jones

2005

Johannes Brahms

and the Twilight
of Romanticism

Johannes Brahms
and the Twilight of Romanticism

Donna Getzinger
Daniel Felsenfeld

**MORGAN
REYNOLDS**
Publishing, Inc.

620 South Elm Street, Suite 223
Greensboro, North Carolina 27406
http://www.morganreynolds.com

B
BRAHMS

Classical Composers

Johann Sebastian Bach

Antonio Vivaldi

Richard Wagner

Johannes Brahms

George Frideric Handel

JOHANNES BRAHMS AND THE TWILIGHT OF ROMANTICISM

Library of Congress Cataloging-in-Publication Data

Getzinger, Donna.
    Johannes Brahms and the Twilight of Romanticism / Donna Getzinger and Daniel
    Felsenfeld.
       v. cm. — (Classical composers)
    Includes bibliographical references (p.) and index.
    Contents: Boyhood in Hamburg — The Whirlwind Tour — Love in D Minor —
City of Dreams — *A German Requiem* — From Sorrow to Symphony — Working
Summers — Farewell.
    ISBN 1-931798-21-4 (library binding)
    1. Brahms, Johannes, 1833-1897—Juvenile literature. 2. Composers—Germany—
Biography—Juvenile literature. [1. Brahms, Johannes, 1833-1897. 2. Composers.] I.
Felsenfeld, Daniel. II. Title. III. Series.
    ML3930.B75G4 2004
    780'.92—dc22

                        2003027115

Printed in the United States of America
First Edition

To Kyla and Teagan,
and to Caylin, who hears Brahms's "Lullaby" every night

Contents

Chapter One
Boyhood in Hamburg

When Johannes Brahms, by this time a well-respected composer, finally bought a home of his own, it was in his adopted hometown of Vienna, Austria in 1871. The modest third-floor apartment was located at No. 4 Karlsgasse. He placed his piano next to the living-room window so that, as he worked on music, he could look out at the Karlskirche next door. Brahms loved to stare out the window at the old church as he painstakingly composed intricate sonatas, songs, serenades, and concertos.

One day Brahms purchased a sculpture, a large bust of the great composer Ludwig van Beethoven (1770-1827), which he had mounted on a shelf over his piano. From then on, Beethoven's relentless eyes stared down at him as he worked. When Brahms struggled with a composition of his own he would pace the small room, and the light from the window would reflect off Beethoven's brooding marble face.

Beethoven's immense shadow loomed over Brahms his entire career. Twenty thousand Viennese had turned out for the master's funeral in 1827. After his death, many believed the world would never again see a composer of such genius. When Johannes Brahms first entered the music world, some twenty-

Ludwig van Beethoven in 1805. *(Courtesy of Malvisi Archive, Populonia.)*

five years later, those music lovers who adhered to traditional forms hoped that he would become Beethoven's successor and carry on in his style. Brahms took this as a great compliment, but also felt the weighty burden of the comparison. He wanted his work to be appreciated because it was uniquely his and feared that, if measured against Beethoven's indisputable genius, his own music would be found forever lacking. By age forty-three Brahms was famous, successful, and prosperous, but he still had not been able to accomplish what would make him the unquestionable heir to Beethoven's legacy. He had not yet mastered the most ambitious of forms, the symphony.

By the spring of 1876, Beethoven had been dead almost fifty years. The last great symphony was twenty-five years old, and its composer, Brahms's old friend Robert Schumann, was also dead. The kind of music Beethoven and Schumann composed was almost out of style. The world was more excited by the works of composers like Franz Liszt and Richard Wagner, who wrote in a new style they boldly called the music of the future.

Over the course of his career, Brahms had written glorious pieces, including his D Minor Concerto and *A German Requiem*. He could spend the rest of his days composing love songs for the many women in his life, or violin concertos for his old and dear friend Joseph Joachim. Brahms's music was played to adoring audiences, and he could continue to grow wealthy from the royalties alone. But beneath the composer's quiet surface was an unfulfilled desire that would not let him rest. There was one more challenge facing him in what had been one of music's most remarkable lives. He wanted to write a symphony that would be heralded as a worthy successor to Beethoven's Ninth, his last and greatest masterpiece.

Johannes Brahms's father had presented him with his first musical challenges. Johann Jakob Brahms had moved to Hamburg from a provincial village in 1827 when he was nineteen. Johann Jakob eked out a living as a small-time musician, fiddling in bars around the working-class districts of the port city. He was self-taught and talented enough to play several instruments, but unable to find a steady job in a respected orchestra. He married Christiane Nissen, a woman eighteen years his senior who worked as a seamstress, in 1830. Eventually Christiane had her own shop.

Johann Jakob Brahms, Johannes's father. *(Courtesy of Bildarchiv der Oesterreichischen National bibliothek.)*

The couple had three children and Johann Jakob hoped each one would be interested in music. The oldest, a daughter named Elise, suffered from migraine headaches and never learned to play, and the youngest, Fritz, learned piano but never showed any exceptional skill. The middle child, Johannes, was born on May 7, 1833, and, not only did he love music with the same enthusiasm as his father, he also revealed a remarkable talent and discipline at an early age.

Johannes had the gift of perfect pitch: he could tell the difference between notes by ear. Before he ever saw a page of written music, he had created his own version of musical notation to write down the songs he invented. His father began teaching him to play violin and cello when he was four, but the boy longed to play the piano.

The modern piano was still a relatively new invention. In Mozart's time, and in the early years of Beethoven's

An early piano.

career, the harpsichord and organ were the most popular keyboard instruments. The organ was cumbersome, expensive, and found primarily in churches. The harpsichord had a tinny sound because its strings were plucked. Although the piano (shortened from the word *pianoforte*) was invented in 1709, it wasn't widely used until the 1800s when the Pleyel Company of France began to develop it. Beethoven influenced the evolution of the piano when he asked the Pleyel Company to give the keyboard a six-octave range, and to include foot pedals to help make the sound resonate. Beethoven preferred the richer sound of the piano to the harpsichord. Because the piano's strings were struck with hammers rather than plucked, the instrument produced a great range of volume and expression in sound simply by the way the keys were touched.

From 1820 to 1850 the piano went through changes in

The Brahms family had a first-floor apartment in this building in Hamburg, which is also the house in which Johannes was born. *(Courtesy of Bildarchiv der Oesterreichischen National bibliothek.)*

size, structure, and design. Different models were made for concert halls and middle-class parlors. As the instrument became more accessible and easier to use, more people wanted one of their own. Pianos became as common as desks and chairs, and piano lessons were considered to be an essential part of a well-rounded education.

If Johannes Brahms had been born into the middle class he would have had access to a piano. But the Brahms family of five lived in a two-room apartment in an area along the waterfront known as "Adulterer's Walk" because of the number of prostitutes that worked the streets. Even after Johannes's father landed a second job playing bass in an ensemble at the ritzy Alster Pavilion, he still could not afford to buy a piano. Furthermore, and more importantly, Johann Jakob did not see how learning to play the piano would benefit his son. If Johannes wanted to be a successful working musician, he would have better luck getting work with the violin or cello. Every band and orchestra needed these instruments. Piano players were not in as high demand.

But it soon became obvious that Johannes was musically gifted, and Johann Jakob was determined to give his son every chance to develop his talent, even if that meant letting him study the piano. He took his son to visit Otto Friedrich Willibald Cossel, who taught piano to many of the wealthier children in Hamburg. At their meeting, Johannes played the cello while his father accompanied him on the bass. By the end of the audition, Cossel was convinced he had discovered a child prodigy. Cossel was eager to take Johannes on as a student and wanted to start lessons right away. Still wary of losing his son to the piano, Johann Jakob told Cossel to teach Johannes to play "as much as you know . . . then he'll know enough."

Young Johannes walked to Cossel's house for lessons and to practice. Once he realized just how talented his young student was, Cossel moved his own family closer to the Brahms home so that Johannes would have easier access to his knowledge and his piano. Johann Jakob eventually bought a cheap upright piano, but it was hard for the boy to concentrate in the small house with his family bustling about, so Brahms did most of his practicing at Cossel's.

Cossel was determined that Brahms would become a piano virtuoso. But Johannes realized that, although he preferred the piano to other instruments, what he really wanted was to become a composer. Just as Johann Jakob had resisted young Brahms's draw to the piano, so Cossel insisted that the boy's learning to write music would be a waste of time. For two years, Cossel trained his protégé in the complexities of the piano. In the process, he gave him a solid grounding in the music of the great composers who had come before him. The music Brahms learned with Cossel would influence his own work for the remainder of his life, and his compositions would demonstrate the debt he felt he owed his musical predecessors.

Brahms's favorite composer, Ludwig van Beethoven, had written in all of the major musical forms, including the opera, concerto, sonata, string quartet, and symphony. Before he went totally deaf, Beethoven was also a renowned pianist who sometimes conducted his own symphonies. His career encompassed the end of the Classical period of Haydn and Mozart, and was critical to the beginning of what has come to be called the Romantic style.

The Classical era, which dates roughly from the mid-1700s to the early 1800s, represented a departure from the elaborately ornamental, dramatic melodies of the Baroque period. Popular composers in the Baroque style include Antonio Vivaldi and Johann Sebastian Bach. In the Classical style the emphasis was on a simpler, more elegant music written according to strict forms.

The beginning of the nineteenth century heralded a new era of rapidly shifting social and economic structures, and great developments and changes were also being made in the arts and sciences. A new appreciation for the individual gained hold over the imagination, and the burgeoning Early Romantic period returned music to a sound that favored emotional expression. Music at this time was often written with a subject, or "program," that dealt with great passions and feelings, in mind. Typical examples are the later compositions of Beethoven, such as his Ninth Symphony of 1823, and the works of Franz Schubert and Felix Mendelssohn.

Mendelssohn was also one of the first composers to make a practice, and eventually a discipline, of studying earlier musicians. Mendelssohn almost single-handedly rediscovered the works of Johann Sebastian Bach, rescuing this great composer from possible oblivion. Soon other composers and students of music were immersing themselves in the great works of the past. Musicians now had a better understanding of music

German composer and pianist Felix Mendelssohn was a key figure in nineteenth-century music. *(Courtesy of Mondadori Archives.)*

history and an appreciation for the ways that compositional style had changed over time. New compositions were enriched by their authors' ability to draw from the wealth of music that had come before. But, on a less positive note, new composers also had to contend with the massive weight of the achievements made by their predecessors. Brahms was a mostly self-educated intellectual who would often spend his last coins on books and manuscripts. From an early age this fiercely competitive and driven composer was aware of the extreme heights his work would have to reach in order to be considered among the greatest.

The week of Johannes's ninth birthday, in 1842, a terrible fire devastated a large section of the city of Hamburg. The Brahms family was spared, but because the city needed to be rebuilt there was little money left for music. All the concerts at the Alster Pavilion, where Johann Jakob worked, were cancelled. The family turned to young Johannes to bring in some money.

Johannes Brahms was presented at his first public performance a year later. He was ten years old when he gave this first recital, where he played pieces by Beethoven and Mozart accompanied by his father on bass. Everyone in attendance was impressed with the young boy who played the piano with as much skill as a grown man.

In the audience that night was an American producer who approached Johann Jakob with the idea of taking Johannes on tour in the United States. The producer was certain that young Johannes would be popular across the ocean, and that he would make a great deal of money. Johann Jakob liked the idea, and Joahnnes's mother promptly sold her shop so the family could prepare to move overseas.

Cossel thought the American tour was a terrible idea. The music world was full of stories of talented children who tried to cash in on their talent but ended up as failures. Johannes had the potential to be a great musician, not

Brahms's second piano teacher, Eduard Marxsen. *(Courtesy of Kurt Hoffman, Hamburg.)*

just a novelty act. But Johann Jakob's mind was made up.

Cossel went to Eduard Marxsen to enlist his help in dissuading Johann Jakob from the American tour. Marxsen had been Cossel's piano teacher. He had decades of experience in the professional music world. If the famous Marxsen agreed to take Johannes on as a student, perhaps Johann Jakob would abandon the idea of touring America. At first Marxsen doubted that Johannes had the potential Cossel claimed. After hearing Johannes play, Marxsen acknowledged the boy's talent but did not believe that his heart was invested in playing the piano. When Cossel mentioned Johannes's interest in composing, though, Marxsen was intrigued. He asked to see something the boy had written. After looking over the pieces, Marxsen realized that Brahms "exhibited a rare acuteness of mind which enchanted me, and, insignificant though his first attempts at original creation turned out to be, I was bound to recognize in them an intelligence which convinced me that exceptional, great, and peculiarly profound talent was dormant in him." Marxsen agreed to take the boy on as a student, and honored him by offering the lessons at no charge. Johann Jakob gave up on the American tour.

Before he began to teach Johannes about musical composition, Marxsen wanted him to have a thorough grounding in the history of music. The work that Cossel had begun was now extended. Marxsen taught him everything he knew about the various forms of music and how they were put together. The precise and elegant structure of Classical era music appealed to Johannes. At the age of eleven he wrote his first piano sonata. (A sonata is a multi-movement piece written for a soloist or an ensemble.) Most Romantic composers rarely wrote in this complicated form, preferring smaller, less-structured pieces that allowed them to convey more feeling. Mendelssohn gave up the sonata when he was eigthtcen, Schumann when he was twenty-six; Frédéric Chopin only wrote three, and Liszt only one. Even Beethoven abandoned the sonata form, but not until he had written thirty-two of them. Marxsen was impressed by his young student's sonata and encouraged him to write more.

As knowledge of earlier music spread, audiences began to prefer hearing performances of the works of past masters instead of premieres of new pieces. This was one of the reasons few major works had been written in recent years. Most of the contemporary music Johannes played and heard indulged the Romantic preference for emotional expres-

A view of Brahms's hometown, Hamburg. *(Courtesy of Arborio Mella.)*

siveness, while avoiding the more demanding forms typical of the Classical era.

While Johannes studied the art of composing, his father

A sketch of Brahms in his youth.

found ways to use Johannes's skill at the piano to make money for the family. At age twelve, he was put to work playing piano in bars near the docks in St. Pauli. These were seedy establishments where sailors drank too much and danced with girls who were paid to entertain the customers. At banged-up old pianos, Johannes played popular songs and dances through the long nights.

As an adult, Brahms would look back at the years he spent working in pubs with shame. "These half-clad girls, to make the men still wilder would take me on their laps between the dances and kiss, caress, and excite me," he remembered. The men forced him to drink beer for their amusement, and many nights Johannes would stumble home drunk in the wee hours of the morning. After a few hours of sleep, he would clean up and go to school where he struggled to pay attention to his lessons. He took to bringing a book to work with him to read while he played. The music he played took little technical effort, but a great emotional toll.

Caught between his serious musical studies and the need to provide money for his family, Johannes lived two lives. By day he studied the intricacies of classical composition; by night he pounded out polkas. During the day his teachers nurtured his talent; at night people shamed him by pouring beer down his throat and forcing him into lewd dances.

Many hours each day were dedicated to his training as a virtuoso; many hours each night were thrown away on drunk and rowdy revelers. His father was careful not to let either Marxsen or Cossel find out about Johannes's evening employment. He knew they would put a stop to it.

Johannes, who had no time for friends or socializing, grew into a sullen and angry teenager, resentful of the burdens his family put on him but unable to find an escape. Small in stature, with boyish good looks and delicate skin, he wore his blond hair below his ears, as was the fashion. It rankled him that, from a distance, he could be mistaken for a young woman. To those who knew him, Johannes could be sarcastic, even caustic; characteristics he would have for the rest of his life. He learned to keep his feelings locked inside, only to be released within the formal constraints of his music. As he grew older, he was unable to relax with eligible women. He did not trust their affections and preferred longing for them from afar to becoming engaged with them on an intimate level.

One of the escapes from the pressures of his life was books. He was particularly fond of Romantic literature, especially the stories of E.T.A. Hoffmann, who was also a composer. Hoffmann's stories were full of magic, intrigue, supernatural happenings, and ample amounts of violence or horror. In some ways he was similar to the American writer Edgar Allan Poe. His stories have been told and retold countless times in several mediums, including by Peter Ilyich Tchaikovsky in his score for the ballet *The Nutcracker* and in movies such as *The Sandman*. One of Hoffmann's leading fictional characters was a reckless young composer named Kreisler, and Brahms took to calling himself by that name. The wild, even mad, Kreisler persona allowed him to express his emotions in a way the more subdued Johannes Brahms could not. Brahms used this alter ego to exorcise his pent-up frustrations and anger.

In 1847, when he was fourteen, Johannes was rescued from playing in pubs. A man named Adolph Giesemann was looking for someone to teach his daughter Lieschen to play piano and Johann Jakob recommended his son for the job. That summer Johannes joined the Giesemann family at their farm in Winsen-an-der-Luhe, a small village not far from his home, but worlds away from his life in the city.

Living in the country, Johannes regained his health and vigor. He enjoyed long afternoon walks in the sunshine after spending mornings teaching piano to Lieschen. They read together under the trees. For the rest of his life, whenever Johannes found himself needing solace or time to think, he would go to the country. Long walks away from the clamor of the city calmed his mind. Kreisler disappeared in the country, and Johannes felt at peace.

While in Winsen, Johannes was asked to conduct the local men's choir. At first the men had trouble taking direction from a mere boy with delicate, almost feminine features and a high-pitched voice. Eventually, though, they saw the quality of his musicianship. He wrote wonderful music for them to sing and improved the quality of their performances so much that they were sad to see him go.

After the first of what would be two summers in Winsen,

Johannes returned to Hamburg. He did not go back to the pubs. He was old enough now to find work in more respectable venues, such as local theaters and restaurants. He also took on some piano students, mostly the overflow from Marxsen's studio. In the fall of 1847, Marxsen decided it was time for Johannes to make his formal debut as a pianist. At fourteen, he was too old to be a child virtuoso like Franz Liszt, Joseph Joachim, or Clara Wieck Schumann, but he was still young enough to cause a stir. Marxsen arranged for him to perform in a chamber music recital on November 20.

That night Johannes performed a piece by a popular composer, Sigismund Thalberg. A few days after the concert an anonymous note appeared in the Hamburg newspaper, commenting on "a little virtuoso called J. Brahms, who not only showed great facility, precision, clarity, power, and certainty, but occasioned general surprise and obtained unanimous applause by the intelligence of his interpretation." This flattering review was actually written by Marxsen in an effort to drum up some interest in his pupil. Other than this mention, the event went unnoticed.

Over the next two years, Marxsen put Johannes in more concert programs. The boy always played well, but no one responded to his music with the applause Marxsen had hoped for. At his last concert, on April 14, 1849, Johannes played one of his own pieces for the first time: "Fantasia for Piano on a Favorite Waltz," a charming and original variation on a popular tune of the day. Though he played his own music with more enthusiasm than he did the work of others, the audience was not moved. They had come to hear the classics, or perhaps to see the next phenomenon in action. They left disappointed.

Marxsen decided it was time to stop trying to promote Johannes as a prodigy and performer. He continued to teach the young man, but now their lessons focused almost exclusively on composing. Johannes was happy. He had never been in-

Brahms pictured with his radical violinist friend Eduard Reményi. *(Courtesy of Kurt Hoffman, Hamburg.)*

terested in becoming a concert pianist—he wanted to write his own music.

Johannes's piano-playing skills did help him to earn some money. He received several offers to accompany touring virtuosos when they gave concerts in Hamburg. In 1850, he played for a violinist who called himself Eduard Reményi and was famous for playing arrangements of Hungarian gypsy music. Two years earlier Reményi, who was both Jewish and Hungarian, had fled his native country as a political refugee. Hungary was part of the Austrian Empire, but Hungarian nationalists, such as Reményi, wanted

Hungary to be sovereign and had started a revolt. When Austria crushed the revolt in 1849, the violinist fled the country to avoid being executed or imprisoned.

Playing with Reményi was a great honor for Brahms. The violinist was well known and had the potential to become world famous. Johannes also loved the sound of the gypsy music, with its intoxicating rhythms and exotic melodies. He would eventually use it, or his Germanic version of it, in his own compositions. The two young men became friends and planned a tour together. Then rumors of his impending arrest sent Reményi fleeing to America.

That same year Robert Schumann, an important and famous composer, came to Hamburg for a concert. Schumann started his career as a piano virtuoso, but after injuring his finger during a hand-strengthening exercise (on a rack-like machine of his own devising) he dedicated the rest of his life to writing music. Schumann was considered to be Franz Schubert's successor in the craft of writing beautiful *lieder* (songs). He expressed in his music the same Romantic sentiments Brahms so enjoyed in literature. Schumann was married to the piano virtuoso

Robert Schumann at thirty years old. *(Courtesy of Bildarchiv preussicher Kulturbesitz.)*

Clara Wieck, who had helped to make her husband's name by playing his pieces at her concerts. Clara had been a famous child prodigy, and while she did not play as often now that she was married and had children, she was still well known, and well loved, by the public.

A friend of Brahms's suggested that he send some of his music to Schumann. In a moment of courage, seventeen-year-old Brahms wrapped up a few of his best compositions and sent them off. Schumann never had time to look at the package and sent it back unopened, which insulted and embarrassed Brahms.

Two of the pieces Brahms sent to Schumann were piano sonatas. These pieces, had Schumann opened them, would certainly have appealed to the master. Capturing the power of youth, the music was full of invention and beautiful melodies, and stretched the sonata form to new lengths.

In December 1852, Reményi returned from America, ready to renew both his friendship with Brahms and their plans for an informal concert tour together. Neither of the musicians was in high demand in Germany, but they thought it would be fun to travel around the country playing wherever they could. Johannes had never been far from home, and was excited about the new experience. That April, just before his twentieth birthday, Johannes left his hometown. He had his father's blessing and promised to write his mother often.

Chapter Two
The Whirlwind Tour

Johannes Brahms and Eduard Reményi had drastically different personalities and often argued during rehearsals, but overall they got along. Reményi was flamboyant. He loved traveling, and happily sailed back and forth across the seas, seeing much of the world. On the other hand, the thought of getting on a boat sent Brahms into a nervous panic. Brahms was a social young man who liked to drink with his friends but afterwards would often feel guilty about his behavior. He was never completely at ease, and often startled his friends with his unpredictable moods.

Despite the fact that Reményi and Johannes played works by Beethoven and other famous composers, as well as the gypsy music, their concerts were poorly attended. Only Hungarian music enthusiasts showed up. Since no-body was paying much attention, they worked some of

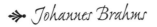

A painting by Anselm Feuerbach depicting gypsy musicians and dancers. Many of Brahms's compositions were influenced by his fascination with this music. *(Courtesy of Hamburger Kunsthalle-Kleinhempel.)*

Brahms's compositions into the program. The tour was not a great success until May, when they went to the city of Hanover in northern Germany. There, Reményi introduced

Brahms to his old schoolmate, Joseph Joachim.

Twenty-two year old Joachim had already achieved fame as a virtuoso violinist. He had been a protégé of Felix Mendelssohn in Leipzig before touring Europe, where he played the great violin concertos of Bach and other masters. Now he was the royal concertmaster (second to the conductor) of the orchestra in Hanover. Like Reményi, Joachim was of Hungarian descent, but that is where the similarity between the two ended. Joachim was very proper and did not approve of Reményi's roguish behavior.

Brahms did not know that Joachim dreaded seeing Reményi again and certainly had little interest in meeting Reményi's touring partner. Brahms was greeted by a stern-faced young man, but he was soon able to turn Joachim's anxiety to delight. Joachim asked Brahms to sit at the piano and perform some of his compositions. Among the pieces he played were his sonatas in C Major and F-sharp Minor and his E-flat Scherzo, three lively and inventive pieces. Joachim was thoroughly im-

Violinist Joseph Joachim developed a great friendship with Brahms. *(Courtesy of Kurt Hoffman, Hamburg.)*

pressed by what he heard, and wrote: "His playing shows that intensive spark, that . . . fatalistic energy and rhythmic precision which prophesy the artist, and his compositions already contain more of finished significance than I have ever encountered in any musical student of his age." Joachim saw what the general public had missed. Brahms performed astoundingly well when playing his own music.

To Brahms's delight, Joachim made it his goal to introduce Johannes Brahms to everyone of musical influence in Hanover. He took genuine pride in his new friend. Reményi often went along on these excursions, but little notice was taken of him. Brahms was the center of attention.

On June 8, 1853, not quite two months since leaving home, Brahms played before Joachim's employer, George V, King of Hanover. The king was so impressed by Brahms that he dubbed him "little Beethoven." It was not the first time Brahms had heard himself compared to Beethoven, nor would it be the last. As always happened when he heard this comparison, Brahms felt the pressure of expectations behind it.

Soon enough, Reményi's politics caught up to him again. Threats of another warrant for his arrest meant he had to leave Hanover. Joachim suggested they go to Weimar, where he could give them a letter of introduction to Franz Liszt. Liszt was one of the most influential composers of the day, and the most famous pianist in Europe. He was also *kapellmeister* (conductor) at the Weimar court, and lived in the ornate palace of Princess Carolyne von Sayn-Wittgenstein. When Joachim was seventeen he had been the concertmaster for Liszt's court orchestra, before moving on to lead his own orchestra in Hanover.

When the two young musicians arrived in Weimar, Brahms was shocked at the extravagance of the palace. He found the excesses outrageous and offensive and felt uncomfortable around Liszt's fancy clothes and confident manners. Overwhelmed by his surroundings, intimidated by Liszt's talent and reputation, Brahms froze when Liszt asked him to play. Famous for being able to play anything on sight, no matter how technically demanding, Liszt took the compositions and played them himself, exquisitely. He then played one of his own compositions. Brahms thought the music reflected its composer: too much ornamentation and too many frills. Brahms cared so little for the music that he fell asleep while Liszt played—a great insult to the famous virtuoso.

Liszt was a founder and proponent of the New German

This 1840 painting shows Franz Liszt at the piano, surrounded by friends, influences, and admirers. *(Courtesy of Photo Archiv für Kunst Geschichte.)*

School, a group of musicians and artists who rejected the traditional forms of music handed down through the Classical and Romantic eras. The members of the New German School sought to make music, poetry, and even the visual arts into a unified whole. Called "program music," their compositions differed from earlier styles because they were written in order to tell a specific story. In fact, proponents of the New German School often claimed that the story had greater importance than the music itself, saying the story depended on the music for its telling, but the music existed only so that the story could be told.

Liszt had recently created a piece of program music titled "Mazeppa." He also invented a new genre he called the symphonic poem. This orchestral work differed from a regular symphony because it had only one long movement, with a cyclical theme, instead of three or four shorter movements, and it took its inspiration from works of great writers of the Romantic era, such as Lord George Byron and Victor Hugo. Liszt would go on to write twelve more symphonic poems. This form of music would become one of the most popular, second only to the opera.

The primary reason Joachim had left his position working for Liszt was because he disliked the new musical style as much as Brahms did. Like Brahms, he favored "absolute music," music that stood on its own, without poetic titles, dramatic narratives, or borrowed philosophical notions. Music for music's sake, in the tradition of the composers they admired, was what concerned Brahms and his new friend.

Absolute music had also been the goal of the early Romantic composers. In the 1700s instrumental music was used primarily as accompaniment for dancing. Then composers including Haydn, Mozart, and Beethoven began writing instrumental music that was so interesting, and lovely, that people wanted to sit and listen to it. The Romantic com-

Piano virtuoso Franz Liszt, founding member of the New German School. *(Liszt Academy of Music, Budapest.)*

posers wanted their music to convey specific emotions and depth of feeling. Composers like Brahms wanted their audiences to interpret the music themselves, to make the music personal to them, instead of allowing the composer to tell them how it should be experienced. In contrast, advocates of the New German School wanted each audience member to hear the precise story or concept the composer set out to convey.

Absolute music and program music are considered to be divergent branches of Romanticism. Bitter feuds often erupted between the two camps, especially in print. Critics of the day tended to endorse one school or the other, and would make nasty remarks about the opposing style. One critic wrote that Liszt's work required too many pamphlets to be understood. On the other hand, critics often called Brahms's work old-fashioned. The public took sides too, rooting for and defending their favorite composers.

Eduard Reményi liked the New German School, or at least he liked being in Liszt's favor, and he wanted to stay in Weimar. Brahms did not want to stay with him, but the tour had failed to make him famous or wealthy and he felt he had no choice. Joachim invited him to come back to Hamburg, and Brahms returned for the rest of the summer.

Now that he had a place to stay, Brahms's problem was money. Joachim was only twenty-two, but he had been touring for years and was already well off financially. He was happy to supply his new friend with money for living expenses, though the arrangement made Brahms's mother uncomfortable. Christiane worried her son would create a debt he could not repay. She wrote, "If you get every little thing from Joachim, you will be under too great an obligation."

Brahms must have showed her letter to Joachim, because the violinist himself wrote to reassure her: "Allow me . . . to write and tell you how infinitely blessed I feel in the companionship of your Johannes. . . . You will understand my wish to have him near me as long as his presence does not interfere with his duty to himself."

After two months with Joachim, Brahms decided to go on a hiking tour along the Rhine River. Though he was slight in stature, Brahms was active and vigorous. His love for the countryside had not abated, and he planned an ambitious hike, carrying all of his supplies on his back. When Joachim learned that Brahms would be passing by Düsseldorf, he

At 820 miles long, the Rhine is Europe's principal waterway. From east-central Switzerland, it flows north and west through Austria, Germany, France, and the Netherlands before emptying into the North Sea.

insisted Brahms stop to call on Robert and Clara Schumann. To make this easier, he gave Brahms a letter of introduction to present to the famous composer, and he wrote a letter to the Schumanns so they would know to expect a visit from his new friend.

Robert and Clara Schumann.
(Hamburger Kunsthalle-Kleinhempel.)

Brahms still believed Schumann to be the self-centered, rude man who had refused to open a package from a struggling artist in search of advice and validation. Joachim tried to dispel that belief, but his words had little effect. When Brahms arrived in Düsseldorf, he lingered for a long time outside the Schumann house before finally knocking on the door. Joachim spoke so highly of Schumann, and Brahms admired the man's music so much, he could not bear to walk away. But as he knocked, he prepared himself for another rejection.

To his surprise, Schumann himself opened the door, still wearing his nightgown. After reading Joachim's letter, he invited the young man into his home. Shyness overtook Brahms, even though the celebrated composer in front of him appeared just as uncomfortable. Since Joachim's letter had praised Brahms as a composer, Schumann asked him to play some of his music. Brahms was not as paralyzed as he had been before Liszt, but he had to take deep breaths to steady his hands. Then he sat down at the piano and began the passionate opening chords of his C Major Piano Sonata.

After only a few bars, Schumann stopped the young man. He went to get his wife, Clara, then indicated that he should begin again. Clara's presence made Brahms even more nervous. Though he had never heard her play, he was well aware of her talent. She did not give concerts often now that she was married and had children, but she was still a revered musician. Clara was nine years younger than her husband and fourteen years older than Brahms. While not conventionally beautiful, her dark blue eyes radiated intelligence, and she had a grace about her that calmed and charmed Brahms. He began again.

Brahms played his music all that afternoon, mostly the same pieces that had impressed Joachim's musical colleagues. The Schumanns offered few comments while they listened. Brahms was unsure whether they enjoyed what they heard or were holding back their criticism out of politeness. However, it was clear that they enjoyed his company, as they invited him to return the following day.

The comments they had not spoken aloud earlier appeared in their diaries that night. Robert Schumann wrote only: "Visit from Brahms (a genius)." Clara wrote a bit more: "Here again is one who comes as if sent from God! He played us sonatas and scherzos of his own, all of them rich in fantasy, depth of feeling and mastery of form. . . . It is truly moving to behold him at the piano, his interesting young face transfigured by the music, his fine hands which easily overcome the greatest difficulties (his things are very difficult), and above all his marvelous works. . . . A great future lies before him."

Brahms, for his part, wrote to Joachim praising Schumann, and lamenting the time he had wasted holding a grudge against the composer.

The next day, worried that their invitation to lunch had been good manners and nothing more, Brahms stayed away. When he did not show, Clara went to town, found Brahms at a small hotel pub, and brought him back to the house. She made sure that he knew he was always welcome in their home, and invited him to stay with them until Joachim arrived later in the month.

The Schumanns' companionship and tutelage inspired Brahms. There were six Schumann children, and Brahms delighted in spending time with them. He was often found cavorting in the garden or doing handstands on the banisters. His music flourished along with his personality. He added three more movements to the F Minor Sonata he had been writing, attempted some chamber music (pieces written for a small number of instruments and played primarily in homes of the wealthy), and wrote several small vocal works for the women's choir that Schumann directed. During this time he also practiced his piano playing under Clara's masterful coaching.

Brahms was extremely happy during his stay with the Schumanns. They had what he, the poor child from the wrong side of Hamburg, had imagined to be the perfect family life—a cozy house, happy children, doting parents, and a great sense of love and stability. The popularity of Robert Schumann's publications and his position as town music director allowed him to work at home most of the time.

Robert Schumann believed artists should cultivate a community of their peers and he encouraged Brahms to form friendships with other composers and musicians, as he had been encouraged to do throughout his own career. *(Courtesy of Niedersächsisches Landesmuseum, Hanover.)*

Schumann, like Joachim before him, was eager to introduce Brahms to his colleagues. One person Brahms met during his stay in Düsseldorf was Albert Dietrich, a well-known local composer and conductor. Brahms and Dietrich were the same age and had similar tastes in music and literature. They struck up an instant and intense friendship. Having close friends was a new experience for Brahms, and he took his new friendships as seriously as his music. The people he met in 1853 and 1854 would remain his closest companions throughout his life. With Dietrich he discussed musical ideas, but also, for the first time, told an outsider about his childhood experiences working in pubs and supporting his family.

As Joachim's arrival neared, Schumann, Dietrich, and Brahms wrote a violin sonata for him to play. A lively and jocular work, the notes of the melody make reference to Joachim's love life. They called the piece the *F.A.E.* Sonata, because those three notes spelled out the German words for "free but lonely." Upon his arrival, amid much hilarity, Joachim was immediately prevailed upon to play the sonata while Clara accompanied him on the piano. As he played his violin, he was asked to guess who wrote which part. It was an easy test for him because their writing styles were so unique; he knew immediately that Dietrich wrote the opening, Schumann the intermezzo (an interlude between the opening and final movement), and Brahms the concluding scherzo (a lively, playful piece, usually in triple time).

Schumann was impressed and greatly pleased with his new houseguest. He wrote an editorial about Brahms for the journal of musical opinion, *Neue Zeitschrift für Musik.* Schumann had founded the journal in 1834, but stopped writing for it when the editors gave their allegiance to Liszt and the New German School. Despite his distance from the journal, Schumann knew they would likely publish anything he submitted.

Title page for the *F.A.E.* Sonata showing Brahms's dedication of the piece to Joachim. *(Courtesy of Bildarchiv preussicher Kulturbesitz.)*

This drawing depicts Joseph Joachim playing violin with Clara Schumann accompanying him on the piano. *(Courtesy of Archiv für Kunst und Geschichte.)*

Schumann's article raved about Brahms: "I thought that . . . there must and would suddenly appear one whose destiny should be to express the spirit of our age in the highest and most ideal fashion. . . . His name is Johannes Brahms; he comes from Hamburg, where he had worked in quiet obscurity, though trained in the most difficult rules of his art. . . . His comrades hail him on his first journey out into the world, where wounds perhaps await him, but laurels and palms besides. We welcome him as a stout figure."

Schumann was well known for exuberantly praising young composers, and few had ever lived up to his predictions. Still, once Brahms read the article, it seemed as though a huge weight had been placed upon his shoulders. He felt he must live up to every word Schumann had written about him, not only because he had so much respect for his mentor but because deep inside he believed those words to be true. Though self-deprecating in public, Brahms was privately ambitious and determined.

In response to Schumann's praise, Brahms wrote to him, "You have made me so immensely happy that I cannot attempt to thank you in words. God grant that my works may soon prove to you how much your affection and kindness and encouragement has stimulated me. The public praise you have bestowed on me will have fastened general expectation so exceptionally upon my performances that I do not know how I shall be able to do some measure of justice to it."

Schumann's public endorsement encouraged two publishers to solicit work from Brahms. Choosing which of his pieces to set into print was not a decision he took lightly. He would never issue anything that he felt was not his best possible work. Joachim told Brahms not to worry so much; in his opinion, all of the young composer's work was worthwhile: "It really seems to me immaterial . . . with which of your works you first declaim to the world. A heavenly vision remains a heavenly vision even if it begins by merely showing the world . . . its big toe."

Ultimately, the publishers made the final choice of which pieces to print. Breitkopf & Härtel took two piano sonatas, a set of six songs, and the E-flat Minor Scherzo, numbering them opuses 1-4. Another publisher, Senff, published a third sonata and another set of songs as opuses 5 and 6.

The German city of Leipzig. *(Courtesy of Museum für Geschichte der Stadt, Leipzig.)*

These publications introduced Brahms as a serious composer. They also reflected a tenderness and intimacy that he must have gained from his new friendship with Schumann. Part of his continuing musical appeal comes from how inventive his compositions are. He sought out new ideas and borrowed from the past, reworking the melodies of Beethoven, Bach, and Haydn into his own.

In November, the Schumanns went to Holland for a tour. Brahms went to Leipzig, where he performed in concert for the first time since Schumann's article and the publication of his music. Many composers from the New German School were in attendance to see Schumann's new genius.

They came full of doubt because Schumann was the staunchest and most vocal member of the "enemy" camp.

One of the New Germans in attendance was Karl Franz Brendel, the editor of the *Neue Zeitschrift*, who wrote a critique of Brahms's performance that suggested Brahms would "someday become what Schumann has predicted of him, an epoch-making figure in the history of art." Brendel's review did little to impress the people of Leipzig, who had no interest in Schumann or his new discovery, but it meant a great deal to Brahms. Combined with that single sentence of praise, Brahms's trip to Leipzig was made worthwhile when he met a like-minded composer named Julius Otto Grimm, who would remain one of his closest friends for many years.

On December 20, 1853, Brahms returned to Hamburg for Christmas. Feeling triumphant after his seven months away, Brahms proudly presented his father with a copy of his first publications.

Chapter Three
Love in D Minor

At the beginning of 1854, Brahms went to Hanover to see Joachim conduct one of Schumann's symphonies. Clara stayed at home with her husband. She was worried about his health. For many years, Robert Schumann had experienced periodic breakdowns. He sometimes heard voices, had trouble interacting with other people, and had several times wandered off, telling those who found him that he had no idea how to get home. For years, Clara had cared for her husband alone.

By February it was obvious Schumann was getting worse. He raved incoherently and several times told Clara that angels were urging him to do something. She brought in doctors, but they were no help. Then one day Schumann bolted from the house and ran into town, wearing only a nightgown. There was a parade and a festival underway, but

The asylum in Endenich where Robert Schumann was sent after his mental health began seriously deteriorating. *(Courtesy of Bibliotheque Nationale, Paris.)*

Schumann made his way through the crowds to the bank of the Rhine, into which he promptly threw himself.

Schumann was pulled out of the river and immediately placed in an asylum in the small town of Endenich. For fear her presence would upset him, Clara was not allowed to see her husband and she was beside herself with grief. Brahms rushed to be at Clara's side as soon as he heard the news. Though he was still a relatively new acquaintance of the Schumanns, he felt loyalty to both Robert and Clara, and wanted to help their children through this difficult time.

Joachim, Grimm, Dietrich, and Clara's mother also came to her aid, but none of them devoted themselves to her to the extent that Brahms did. Clara appreciated Brahms's attention, favoring him above all of her other friends. "That good Brahms always shows himself a most sympathetic

An 1853 sketch of Clara Schumann. She struggled with the decision to place her husband in an institution. *(By J.B. Laurens, courtesy of Bibliothèque Inguimbertine, Carpentras.)*

friend," she wrote in her diary. "He does not say much, but one can see in his face, in his speaking eye, how he grieves with me. . . . Besides, he is so kind in seizing every opportunity of cheering me with anything musical."

During this stressful period, Clara was pregnant with her eighth child. Brahms moved in nearby, intending to stay until the child was born and Schumann could return home. Brahms donated all the money from his recent publications to the family. It was not nearly enough to live on, however, and Clara had to go back to working full time. Two days after Schumann left for the hospital, Clara, five months pregnant, began teaching lessons and playing concerts. Playing music was actually not difficult for her at this emotional time. She enjoyed letting the music composed by her husband or Brahms wash over her, and as she played her anxiety lifted. She wrote, "I lose myself in it; it moves my whole heart . . . But when I finish playing my anguish is redoubled."

Brahms, too, immersed himself in music, composing at a furious pace during these difficult months. He worked on his D Minor Sonata for Two Pianos and wrote sixteen variations (music in which the composer reworks a tune while maintaining some of the original elements) on Schumann's *Bunte Blätter* (Mottled Leaves). He wrote fourteen of the variations in less than a month. Brahms did not like to perform but, since they needed money, he followed Clara's example and began giving concerts. The two performed together a number of times and played some of Brahms's compositions, which helped to introduce his work to the public.

Between composing and tending to the Schumann children, Brahms spent time in Robert Schumann's study. The Schumanns owned an impressive library of works, including compositions by Bach, Beethoven, Mendelssohn, and Mozart, and Brahms studied these masterpieces, taking them apart to better understand how they were constructed. He came away from his studies invigorated, deciding to rework his D Minor Sonata into a symphony. He would expand the music he had written for two pianos into a piece for full orchestra.

The symphony was considered to be the most difficult

Wolfgang Amadeus Mozart, child prodigy and prolific composer. In his relatively short life he composed numerous operas, symphonies, and chamber pieces. *(Courtesy of Internationale Stiftung Mozarteum, Salzburg.)*

form of music a composer could attempt, but in the 1800s it was still a fairly recent development. In the mid-1700s, Franz Joseph Haydn had begun to write chamber orchestra pieces that differed from the instrumental music of the time in that they were not written to accompany dancing. He wrote more than one hundred symphonies that took the sonata form and expanded it. Although his are shorter than the symphonies to come out of the Romantic era, he is credited with establishing the form. Wolfgang Amadeus Mozart wrote forty-one symphonies and, particularly with his final three, raised the form to an even higher level. Since Mozart, symphonies have become the composer's proving ground.

Brahms knew the sonata form well, but he had no practical experience writing for a full orchestra, which means writing individual scores for each instrumental section as well as soloists. He also had limited experience listening to symphonies. It took money to attend concerts and there had been precious little of that during his childhood. Making the D Minor Sonata into a symphony would turn out to be much more difficult than he had thought. He simply was not yet ready to write a major piece.

On June 11, Clara gave birth to her eighth child. She named the boy after Felix Mendelssohn, who had died six years earlier and was one of Schumann's closest friends. She asked Brahms to be Felix's godfather. This happy occasion was marred by bad news as the doctors at Endenich concluded that Schumann would have to remain in the asylum indefinitely. None of the family were allowed visit him. Little Felix would never meet his father.

Schumann's absence was almost unbearable for Clara, but she found comfort in Brahms's company. As for Brahms, his admiration for Clara, the wife of his friend, continued to deepen. He wrote to Joachim: "I believe that I do not respect and admire her so much as I love her and am under her spell. Often I must forcibly restrain myself from just quietly putting my arms around her and even—I don't know, it seems to me so natural that she would not take it ill."

Clara too felt the stirrings of love, but she hid her feelings, even from herself. She referred to her tenderness toward Brahms as motherly, or sisterly, love. Their correspondence was written in the informal, intimate tone usually reserved for lovers, but she never went so far as to tell him outright how greatly he moved her. She could not as long as her husband, who she loved so much, was still alive.

The surviving letters between Clara and Brahms reveal their deep affection and intense feelings for one another.

Six of the eight Schumann children. They are, from left to right, Ludwig, Marie, with Felix on her lap, Elise (standing), Ferdinand, and Eugenie.
(Courtesy of Robert Schumann Haus, Zwickau.)

When Clara was touring, Brahms joined her as often as he could. He wrote countless musical love notes, and gave them to her with the strict instructions to play them only when she was alone. She gained strength from his devotion and steadfast support.

By November of 1854, Schumann was lucid enough to remember his wife, and he began writing her letters and receiving hers in return. Clara wrote to him of Brahms's devotion to her and their children, and of the lovely variations he had written on Schumann's music. Schumann was thrilled that Brahms was taking care of his wife. "Thank you . . . my dear Johannes, for all your kindness to my Clara. She speaks of it constantly in her letters," he wrote to Brahms. Schumann never displayed any jealousy, only love and gratitude. He even asked for a portrait of Brahms to hang in his hospital room.

Over the following year, Robert Schumann's health continued to decline. Brahms visited the older composer as often as his own performance schedule allowed. Together they went for long walks in the city of Bonn, sometimes visiting Beethoven's grave. (In 1888 his remains were moved to the Central Cemetery of Vienna.) Brahms felt a deep respect and appreciation for Schumann and was sad to see him not in full possession of his faculties. He was glad Clara was spared knowing how ill her husband was.

During this time, Brahms worked diligently at his compositions. He produced an enormous amount of music, but despite his best efforts, was unable to convert his D Minor Sonata into a symphony. Frustrated, he decided to try

A page from Brahms's piano concerto manuscript.

something less ambitious—a piano concerto, a work for a piano soloist accompanied by a full orchestra. A piano concerto seemed within his reach, but it would be another two years before Brahms would complete it.

As Schumann languished in the asylum, Brahms and Clara traveled a good deal and their relationship intensified. Brahms did his best to control his emotions, but it was very difficult for him to love Clara without telling her how he felt. He tried to express his feelings a few times in letters, and she always responded gently, but firmly, that her husband was still alive. A romance with Brahms was unthinkable.

Soon, Brahms moved into the Schumann house, which doubtless gave rise to gossip about the nature of their relationship. But Clara was a popular public figure and many people sympathized with her difficult situation, supporting seven children alone, her husband institutionalized. There may have been whispers about the handsome young man in her house, but nothing ever came of those rumors.

In July of 1856, Robert Schumann reached the end. For several months he had starved himself and now he was

This photograph of Robert Schumann is from 1850, when the composer was forty years old and a few years before he was institutionalized. Schumann reputedly feared from an early age that he would go mad. Througout his career he experienced periods of elated creativity alternating with intense bouts of melancholy. *(Courtesy of Archiv für Kunst und Geschichte.)*

dying. The hospital permitted Brahms to bring Clara for her first and only visit with her husband. It was a painful experience. Schumann was barely conscious. Clara sat by his bed and comforted him as best she could. Brahms looked on, helpless. Schumann died the following day. A few days later, Brahms wrote, "To me Schumann's memory is holy. The noble, pure artist forever remains my ideal. I will hardly be privileged ever to love a better person."

Clara and Brahms brought Schumann's body home and buried him. He had been lost to them for two years and now he was gone forever. Soon after the funeral, Clara and

Brahms took a trip, with several of her children and Brahms's sister, to Switzerland. It is impossible to know what passed between the couple during that time away, but when they returned, Brahms immediately moved his belongings out of her home and back to Hamburg.

Clara might have expected Brahms to propose marriage while they were in Switzerland. Perhaps Brahms, a young man, uncertain of his future, balked at the idea of assuming responsibility for a large family. Or maybe Clara's memories of her husband made her feel too guilty to continue her close association with Brahms. Perhaps he removed himself from her presence so as not to cause her more grief. Perhaps Brahms, who would never marry, was only able to love those women who were unattainable. No matter what happened in Switzerland, Clara and Brahms would remain the closest of friends, visiting and writing each other for the rest of their lives. Brahms would love other women, but in the end, he would always come back to Clara, and she would always be there for him.

Brahms spent the following year in Hamburg finishing his D Minor Concerto and trying to find pleasure in life now that he was apart from Clara. He was still learning about composition, and needed help from his friends to finish the orchestration for his concerto. Though he had an excellent ear for melodies, he was not yet comfortable writing for all the instruments a major work required.

The D Minor Concerto was difficult for Brahms, but stands today as one of his finest accomplishments. Its tumultuous opening, full of anguish and drama, reflects the pain and loss of his past few years. The middle section is, as Brahms promised, a loving and tender ode to Clara. The finale gave Brahms a great deal of trouble, but he eventually brought it to a satisfactory conclusion by using echoes of Beethoven's C Minor Piano Concerto. While the finale is not as strong as the first two movements, the overall effect of the work is powerful. Brahms would not attempt a work of this scale for another fifteen years.

In September of 1857, based on Clara Schumann's recommendation, twenty-four year old Brahms was offered a position at Detmold, a village fifty miles south of Hanover. There, in the court of Leopold II, Brahms conducted the women's choir and gave music lessons to Princess Frederike. The job paid very well, and despite his dislike for royalty, Brahms appreciated the beautiful country setting of the court and enjoyed his long walks almost as much as the opportunity to conduct the court orchestra, which he did whenever the kapellmeister would let him.

The Romantic era marked a change in how orchestras were run. Previously, the composer of the music would also conduct the orchestra as they played it. But as musical scores became more complicated and orchestras became larger, it took someone with special skills to direct all the musicians, interpret the music, and oversee rehearsals—professional conductors became commonplace. Some composers still conducted their own works, but each major orchestra now had its own permanent director, and a composer's presence was by invitation or special appearance only. Some composers, such as Carl Maria von Weber, actually gave up writing music to take on the more stable profession of conducting.

Weber and Felix Mendelssohn were the first conductors to use batons to help the musicians keep time. Batons are thin, wand-like, about a foot long, and light in color in order to be visible. Hector Berlioz came up with the idea of putting the conductor on a podium in front of the orchestra

The famous German composer Carl Maria von Weber. *(Courtesy of Nationalgalerie, Berlin.)*

in order to be more easily seen by the musicians. Eventually, orchestra direction was considered such a skilled position that it became a course of study, and people would dedicate their careers to learning the craft.

For Brahms, the opportunity to work with an established orchestra was quite a privilege. He became more preoccupied than ever with his appearance. Considered by many a handsome man, his short stature, delicate features, and high-pitched voice had always bothered him. His voice had never changed much, even after going through puberty, and he thought it made him seem weak and unmanly. He developed the habit of thrusting his lower lip forward to make his appearance more severe, and he deliberately stressed his

Brahms around time he met Joachim. The two musicians carried on a great friendship and encouraged each other's progress over the years.

voice to try to change its timbre. While working with the chorus, he would yell his directions at the singers. He did vocal exercises and began smoking cigars. He succeeded in getting a scratchier tone, though his voice would still break whenever he raised it.

Borrowing the idea from a game that Schumann and Clara had played while they were engaged, Brahms and Joachim decided to send each other compositions they were working on once a week. The challenge kept them writing and allowed them to offer opinions on the other's works in progress. "Why shouldn't we two intelligent and serious people teach one another better than some professor could?" Brahms wrote to his friend. If one of them failed to send music, he had to pay a small fine, which the other was to use for buying books. Brahms got to buy many more books than Joachim.

The musical season in Detmold lasted four months. Brahms would return for the next two years, but for now he was free to go back to Hamburg. His family had moved into a larger house there, and they offered him the most spacious room. He resolved to stay there for the rest of his life, composing and living the kind of stable existence denied the touring musician. For that reason, Brahms was reluctant to accept an invitation to spend his summer in the German town of Göttingen, but after much cajoling from Clara and Otto Grimm (Brahms's old friend, who taught music there) he finally decided to join them.

One of the singers in Grimm's choir was an attractive young soprano, Agathe von Siebold. Brahms was taken by her lovely voice and good humor. The summer was a time of work as well as pleasure, beautiful music as well as fun

Brahms's one-time fiancée, Agathe von Siebold. *(Courtesy of Kurt Hoffman, Hamburg.)*

and games. Brahms made merry with his friends and composed love songs for Agathe, which were eventually published in Opus 14. He also wrote music for the ancient prayer *Ave Maria* that evoked the sound of Renaissance music from three hundred years earlier. Agathe's women's choir sang the piece to much acclaim. Today there are many versions of the *Ave Maria,* and Brahms's is among the best known.

Brahms's flirtation with Agathe caused increasing tension between him and Clara, tension that reached its peak when she caught Brahms and Agathe in an embrace. The next day, Clara packed her bags and fled Göttingen. She and Brahms would eventually reconcile, but there was more trouble for the two of them yet to come.

In January 1859, Brahms went to Hanover, where Joachim was preparing to conduct the premiere of Brahms's D Minor Concerto. On his way, Brahms stopped at Göttingen to see Agathe, and while he was there the couple became engaged, most likely at Grimm's urging and to protect Agathe's reputation. The news was to be kept secret, but it soon leaked out. Brahms would eventually break the engagement in a painful and embarrassing fashion, but not before the D Minor Concerto was played.

The piece had weaknesses, and Brahms went to Hanover aware that it might not be received well. His spirits were lifted by the dress rehearsal, and though the audience at the concert did not hate the music, they certainly did not love it. The concerto was unlike those they were used to hearing and, while they could feel the power of the music, they were not sure how to respond.

The concerto was next performed in Leipzig, the home of the New German School. Not only did the audience withhold their applause between movements, they actually booed and hissed when the performance ended. Brahms's failure in Leipzig was not unexpected. He was on the territory of his musical enemies and, as a local critic had once written, "new works do not succeed in Leipzig."

Brahms was casual about the negative reception when he reported the event to Joachim: "The failure has made no impression whatever on me. . . . I believe this is the best thing that could happen to one; it forces one to concentrate on one's thoughts and increases one's courage. After all, I'm only experimenting and feeling my way as yet. But the hissing was too much of a good thing, wasn't it?"

Though he tried to appear nonplussed, Brahms was wounded that his concerto had not made a more positive impact. Soon after this failure, he broke off his engagement to Agathe in a letter, saying he could love her but could not marry her. He would later explain that his hesitation to marry came from fear: "if. . . I had had to meet the anxious, questioning eyes of a wife with the words 'another failure'—I could not have borne that." Though he would not admit it, his breakup with Agathe was another example of how he would flee any relationship that became too intimate. He was not comfortable getting too close to a woman. Throughout his life, he frequented the same type of brothels he had played the piano in as a boy. He sometimes seemed to be ashamed that he preferred this sort of activity to a more long-lasting relationship, but he was apparently unable to

maintain sexual intimacy with women he loved and respected.

A few months later, in March of 1859, Brahms finally
had some success with his concerto. It was performed to a
sold-out crowd in Hamburg and the hometown audience
warmly applauded the composer's efforts. Proud of this
small victory, he wrote his A Major Serenade and quickly
followed it with another, this time in D Major. (Serenades
are often love songs, and are usually preformed outside in
the evening.) The salary he had earned for his concerto
allowed him to donate some time to the women's choir
conducted by Karl Grädener. Nearly all the women there
developed crushes on the handsome composer, and Brahms
admired several of them in return.

This success could not erase the memories of his failure
in Leipzig, though. Brahms wrote to Joachim, "My fingers
often itch… to write anti-Liszt articles." He wanted to take
on the New German School and its adherents by challenging
their leader, Franz Liszt. Together, Brahms and Joachim
wrote a short article condemning the music of their rivals
and the fact that the music journal *Neue Zeitschrift für Musik*
would only endorse music by those affiliated with the New
German School.

Brahms and Joachim intended to pass the article around
to at least two dozen of their allies, including Clara, who
would sign their names in agreement at the bottom. But
someone got a copy of the article after only four people had
signed it and sent the pages to a magazine in Berlin, the
Echo. What Brahms had intended to be a scathing indict-

ment from a large group of respected musicians came off instead as a foolish and petty attack from a handful of jealous artists. A parody of his manifesto appeared before the original made it into print, and the rift between the two schools grew ever wider.

In an effort to redeem himself in the public eye, Brahms returned to his compositions with a vengeance. In April of 1861, just before his twenty-eighth birthday, he decided not to return to Detmold for the summer. Instead, he moved from his parents' home to a suburb just outside of Hamburg. He wanted nothing to distract him from his music.

A cartoon depicting the exuberant Franz Liszt in concert. *(Courtesy of Bulloz.)*

The Hellmesberger Quartet, which premiered a number of Brahms pieces, including his G Minor Piano Quartet with Brahms joining them on piano. *(Courtesy of Historisches Museum der Stadt, Vienna.)*

Two works to come out of 1861 were the G Minor and A Major Piano Quartets, Brahms's earliest attempts at chamber music. He also finished some variations on a theme by George Frideric Handel for solo piano. Handel was a German composer from the Baroque period and had been a contemporary of Bach. A music publisher, Friedrich August ("Fritz") Simrock, befriended Brahms, and at Brahms's request took over all of his business affairs, including his accounting. Brahms explained once to Clara, "Every New Year he sends me an account, which I sign, without, of course, reading or understanding a syllable of it." His trust was complete, and Fritz never took advantage of it.

Hamburg had always been Brahms's hometown, and he hoped it would be the place where he would finally settle down with a permanent position and a family. When the conductor of the Hamburg Philharmonic retired, Brahms made it known that he wanted the job. He did not have much conducting experience, but he was sure his fame and popularity would give him an edge over any other applicants.

While waiting for news from the Hamburg Philharmonic, Brahms took a vacation, assuming there would be little time for travel after he began work. He went south to Vienna, Austria, the farthest he had ever been from his home in Northern Germany. For a musician, there was no better destination. Vienna had been home to the greatest composers of all time, including Haydn, Mozart, Beethoven, and Franz Schubert. Brahms was in this musical city when he received word that the conducting position in Hamburg had been given not to him, but to his friend Julius Stockhausen.

Brahms was furious, broken-hearted, and jealous. Sympathetic letters from his friends Joachim and Clara helped him get through this emotional setback. As well, the wonderful success of his G Minor Quartet (performed in Vienna just two nights before receiving the bitter news) and the beautiful Austrian city itself helped to lessen the blow. Feeling slighted by Hamburg, Brahms decided he would stay on in Vienna indefinitely. He had no reason to go home.

Chapter Four
City of Dreams

The Viennese adored everything about music, including the people who wrote and played it. Statues of composers from earlier generations lined the avenues, and plans for new concert halls and opera houses were always being drawn up. Most people could play some instrument reasonably well, and evenings were spent dancing to waltzes and playing piano arrangements in the parlors.

In Vienna, Brahms was not isolated from other musicians of merit as he had been in Hamburg. He could always find a cheery musical event to attend, and because the city was the most cosmopolitan place in Central Europe, all of his friends would come there sooner or later, to play concerts or just to visit. Brahms loved the Viennese cafés, with their heavy food, thick coffee, and intellectual conversations. Some of the older people in the city had known Beethoven

A view of one of Vienna's parks.

and Schubert personally, and he enjoyed listening to their stories. The many taverns that lined the Ringstrasse (a broad avenue that circles central Vienna and contains many statues, museums, theaters, and concert halls) provided wonderful locations for late night parties, drinking, and dancing.

Among Brahms's favorite places in Vienna was the famous park known as the Prater. The land had originally been set aside so the Austrian emperor could go hunting in solitude and had since been turned into a city park full of cafés, theaters, and beer halls. There were enough trees and grass to recreate the feel of the countryside Brahms loved, but there were also plenty of people who recognized and admired the composer as he strolled along the paths. At night, he could go to the taverns along the park and listen to music provided by the local Ladies' Orchestra, or sip coffee at the Café Czarda and hear the gypsy bands. In a letter to Julius Otto Grimm, Brahms announced:

> Yes, so it goes! I have settled in, I live here ten paces from the Prater and can drink my wine where Beethoven drank his. It is also quite jolly and pretty here, so that it really couldn't be any better. Of course, to wander around the Black Forest with a wife as you do is not only jollier, but more beautiful too.

As much as he loved his life in Vienna, Brahms still longed for the stability and permanence that his friend had.

Always initially charming (his characteristic crassness and irritability came out once he was comfortable with someone), Brahms began to make influential friends, including Eduard Hanslick, the music critic for Vienna's major newspaper, *Die Presse.* Hanslick and Brahms got on famously because the journalist was a great supporter of the old school of Romantic music. He had written passionately about the music of Robert Schumann and made clear his distaste for the New German School. In fact, Hanslick was most famous for publishing a book called *On Beauty in Music,* which praised composers like Brahms, who still used the old forms, over composers like Richard Wagner and Liszt, who wrote program music.

Hanslick's ideas made him unpopular in some circles. Wagner even named a villain in one of his operas after him, which was fitting, since Hanslick made clear at every opportunity his distaste for Wagner's operas. Some thought Hanslick was too conservative and that he used his influence to ensure that traditional music was favored over newer styles. For Brahms, though, Hanslick was the perfect friend and ally—someone who could help him get more of his music performed.

The influential music critic Eduard Hanslick. *(Courtesy of Kurt Hoffman, Hamburg.)*

At the time, there were two important orchestras in Vienna: the Opera/Philharmonic (which would later become the Vienna Philharmonic, an institution still active and vital today) and the Gesellschraft der Musikfreunde (Society of the Friends of Music). Otto Dessoff conducted the Philharmonic, and Johann Herbeck conducted the Gesellschraft. Between the two groups, seventeen professional orchestral concerts were presented each year, and Brahms attended as many of them as possible. Eventually he became friendly with both conductors, and they added Brahms's compositions to their performance schedules.

It did not take long for Brahms to become a major figure in Vienna's musical scene. Within a few months he was playing piano publicly again, thanks to another new friend, Julius Epstein, who was the city's top pianist. Though

Brahms thought of himself mainly as a composer, Vienna seemed to be more receptive to hearing him play the piano, especially if he played pieces by other composers. When he played his own music the reaction was usually cool, but they loved his renditions of Bach, Schumann, Beethoven, and Mozart. Aside from these concerts and a few publications, Brahms supported himself by teaching piano lessons.

Not all of Brahms's music was ignored in Vienna. His G Minor Piano Quartet was played to great acclaim. For the first part of the performance the crowd seemed unmoved, but the final movement—a gypsy-like dance inspired by Brahms's old friend Reményi and by the music he heard in Vienna's cafés—brought the audience to their feet. In the same week, Johann Herbeck conducted Brahms's D Major Serenade, and though the performance was flawed, the crowd responded positively.

Brahms spent Christmas of 1862 alone. He did not go home to visit with his family, nor did he travel to be with Clara Schumann. Instead, he prepared for his second major Viennese solo concert and worked on new compositions, including his Paganini Variations.

Niccolò Paganini (1782-1840) had been a popular Italian composer and violin virtuoso. Much of his energetic music focused on folk and gypsy styles, which matched his outrageous and eccentric lifestyle. His music was so expressive that he was rumored to be in league with the devil. Brahms wrote his variations on Paganini's music to explore how a piano might recreate the sound of Paganini's violin. Clara did not particularly like the Paganini Variations, but she enjoyed the challenge of playing the complicated music, which she affectionately dubbed the "Witch's Variations." Karl Tausig, a talented pianist and friend of Brahms, was the first to debut the variations in concert, and he wrote of the experience, "I had a devil of a time with them. . . . Everybody considers them unplayable, yet secretly they nibble at them, and are furious that the fruits hang so high."

In January 1863, at the age of twenty-nine, Brahms gave a solo recital. Richard Wagner was in the audience and was impressed with the performance. Wagner had revolutionized nineteenth-century opera by combining musical, poetic, and scenic elements into grand displays. Because he believed operas should be complete dramatic works, he was included in the New German School, but his talent and

Charasmatic and wildly talented, Niccolò Paganini was rumored to have made a pact with the devil. *(Courtesy of The Royal College of Music, London.)*

The revolutionary German composer Richard Wagner. His ideas about music contrasted sharply with those of Brahms. *(Photograph by F. Hanfstaengl, Munich.)*

vision far surpassed the other members. Although he disagreed with Wagner's theories, Brahms thought his operas were astounding.

The two composers met several times over the years. Oddly, it was Wagner, the older composer, who favored new and inventive music, while Brahms, the younger composer, favored the old styles. While he would not admit to admiring traditional music, Wagner said of Brahms, "One sees what may still be done in the old forms when someone comes along who knows how to use them." Once, Wagner invited Brahms to play for him at his Vienna dwellings. The two composers would battle over theory throughout their careers but still admired each other's work immensely.

No matter how busy Brahms was, or how many friends he made in Vienna, he always felt as though he was on his own, never quite settled or happy. In February 1863, Joachim informed Brahms that he was engaged to Amalie Wiess, a successful opera singer. Brahms wrote an enthusiastic letter to his old friend, calling him a "lucky fellow" and saying that he looked forward to the time when he could "bend over a cradle" at Joachim's house. The letter also revealed some of Brahms's pain at not yet having found a wife of his own when he wrote: "I must guard against dreams of another kind . . . And then you turn up and pluck the ripest and most beautiful apple in Paradise for yourself!"

Only Clara, who was so often torn away from her children and the structured life she preferred, could possibly understand how much Brahms longed for permanence. He wrote to her of his sadness, "How seldom does someone like us find a fixed abode, how I would have liked to find it in my native city. Now here [in Vienna], where so much beauty delights me, I nevertheless feel and would always feel I am a stranger and can find no peace."

Brahms received word in April of 1863 that his mother, Christiane, was depressed and sick. She was forcing his father to practice his music in the cold, damp attic because the noise disturbed her and aggravated Elise's migraine headaches. Johann Jakob, in turn, threatened to move out and abandon his wife and daughter. In an attempt to mend the problems with his family, Brahms went home in May.

He rented an apartment in Hamburg, unsure about how long he would stay. Regardless of the uncertainty of his situation, he began to work, and wrote a cantata (similar to an opera, but without sets, costumes, or staging) called *Rinaldo*. His interest in theatrical music had been sparked by the work of Franz Schubert, an Austrian composer from the early Romantic age. In particular, Brahms was enchanted by Schubert's Easter cantata *Lazarus*. *Rinaldo* was

Composer Franz Schubert (above), like Brahms, drew inspiration from the gypsy music common throughout Eastern Europe. *(Osterreichishce National bibliothek, Vienna.)*

his attempt to pay homage to Schubert. Having only recently been in Wagner's company, it may also have been Brahms's first attempt to compete with Wagner's operas. Around the same time, Wagner toyed with writing a symphony, perhaps just to compete with Brahms.

While in Hamburg, Brahms visited the women of his old choir, and even wrote them some short pieces. He settled into routines but could not quite feel comfortable with the decision to stay in Hamburg and resume his old life. He had yet to make a name for himself, and in his eyes he had come back to Hamburg a failure.

Before long, Vienna beckoned him back. Brahms received news that he had been offered a job as conductor of the Singakademie, one of the two amateur choral groups in Vienna. The Singverein, the other important group, had long overshadowed the Singakademie. When the Singakademie's conductor died, they hired Brahms with the hope that he could help make them more competitive.

Brahms took some time before responding to the offer. He had to weigh the benefits of taking a permanent job over giving up the free time he had for composing. Finally, in an official letter to the committee accepting the post, he wrote, "that your choice as conductor of the Wiener [Vienna] Singakademie could have fallen to me is a mark of confidence that surprises as much as it honors me, and which I cherish gratefully."

Brahms returned to Vienna in August 1863, and gave his first concert with the Singakademie in November, conducting music by Bach, Schumann, and the Renaissance composer Heinrich Issak. Brahms took this concert very seriously, dedicating all of his energy to creating an impressive program and to making sure the singers were up to the job. He even wrote a special organ part for the Bach piece that helped the singers consistently hit their notes. The concert was an all-out success.

Brahms went on to conduct the Singakademie in more challenging pieces, such as Bach's *Christmas Oratorio* and *St. John Passion,* as well as a concert of his own music. Most of the concerts were well received, and Brahms's fame as a conductor grew. But he was not necessarily happy. Being a conductor required planning rehearsals, assigning parts, teaching the music, putting up posters for concerts, attending meetings with other faculty members, worrying about singers falling ill, and other administrative responsibilities to which he was not well suited.

Another problem was that Brahms kept falling in love with members of his chorus. He planned to ask one of the singers, Ottile Hauer, to marry him. He went to her house in January 1864, only to find she was already engaged. He wrote ruefully to Clara Schumann, calling Ottile "a very pretty girl with whom God knows I might have made a fool of myself if, as luck would have it, someone had not snatched her up at Christmas."

Not long after that embarrassment, Brahms took on a pretty blond piano student named Elisabet von Stockhausen (no relation to Brahms's friend Julius). After a few lessons, Brahms confessed that he would fall in love with her if they continued. He recommended her to another teacher. Elisabet eventually married another, but remained close friends with Brahms for the rest of her life, even if, at times, she was jealous of Brahms's attention to Clara Schumann.

In 1864, after only one season, Brahms quit his job at the Singakademie. He had become a popular conductor, but felt too tied down by the business end of the position. Free from job and relationship commitments, Brahms had time to focus on family matters at home. He had tried to prevent his parents from breaking up by using his influence to get his father a more prestigious and better-paying job with the Hamburg Philharmonic Orchestra. No longer a struggling musician trying to make a living playing in bars, Johann

Jakob was now a proper member of the middle class. Unfortunately, the new job did not solve the problems between Brahms's parents, and Johann Jakob soon left his wife and daughter.

After the breakup, Johann Jakob enjoyed himself emotionally and financially, but Christiane and Elise did not fare so well. Christiane was in her seventies and Elise was always ill, so they had no way of supporting themselves. Brahms did what he could to help his mother

Elisabet von Stockhausen was a student of Brahms's for only a short time. They would, however, remain lifelong friends. *(Courtesy of Kurt Hoffman, Hamburg.)*

and sister but had little money of his own to spare.

Rather than spend the summer of 1864 in Vienna or return to the gloom that awaited him in Hamburg, Brahms decided to visit the resort city of Baden-Baden near the Black Forest. Clara was staying in a small cottage there with her children. Brahms stayed in a hotel nearby. He played music and ate at the Schumann household daily and, through Clara, met important people who would help his career.

Baden-Baden was one of the most fashionable places to

visit in Europe, and many people of note made their summer pilgrimages there. Brahms lunched with Pauline Viardot-Garcia, an extremely talented pianist, singer, composer, teacher, and painter. She had retired from the stage and taught voice lessons in Baden-Baden. One of her good friends was the Russian writer Ivan Turgenev. Famous for his play *A Month in the Country* and his novel *A Nest of Gentlefolk,* and known for his poetic realism and skillful characterization, Turgenev was a peer of the great Russian writers Fyodor Dostoevsky and Leo Tolstoy. Together, Brahms, Viardot-Garcia, and Turgenev passed time by writing short operatic pieces and performing them for friends.

Brahms also met Johann Strauss the Younger, composer of the *Blue Danube Waltz*. Brahms was so impressed by the work that he told Strauss he would give everything he owned to have written it himself, and under the title on a copy of the piece he wrote "not, alas, by Brahms."

The most important person Brahms met that summer, however, was the conductor Hermann Levi, recently appointed kapellmeister at Karlsruhe, where he conducted both orchestra concerts and operas. Hermann Levi had a wonderful sense of humor and quickly became one of Brahms's closest friends.

Levi was Jewish and a rabbi's son. At this point in history, many in Germany and Austria had mixed feelings about Jewish people. Wagner was one of the leading voices against them. He had published an essay entitled "Judaism in Music," which argued that Jews were holding German music back from reaching its potential level of greatness.

Austrian composer Johann Strauss the Younger, conducting.

Wagner became infamous for his anti-Semitism. Levi was not only Jewish, but he had not converted to Christianity, something expected of Jews if they wanted to succeed in the music world of the nineteenth century. Brahms, always Wagner's opposite, sympathized with Jewish people and rejected the developing anti-Semitic movement.

Seeking advice, Brahms asked Levi to look at the manuscripts of his first three piano sonatas. Levi, who was much more experienced with orchestration than Brahms, tried to convince him to turn his F Minor Sonata for Two Pianos into an orchestral work. But Brahms was reluctant to attempt another work of that scale and he resisted his friend's suggestion. Instead, he continued to learn from Levi until he felt the time was right to attempt such a major project again.

That summer in Baden-Baden Brahms was very happy.

The title page from a piano edition of a Strauss waltz, dedicated to Brahms. *(Courtesy of Weiner Stadt und Landesbibliothek.)*

He enjoyed spending time with Clara and her children, but the news of Joachim's engagement made him wonder if he had made a mistake in breaking off his relationship with Agathe. His friend Otto Grimm had stopped speaking to him over the breakup, which he and others thought was a terrible mistake. Now Brahms wondered if they were right.

At the summer's end, Brahms went to visit Otto Grimm in Göttingen. Grimm thought Brahms was coming to patch up their friendship, but Brahms used the trip to revisit places he had enjoyed in Agathe's company, pining away for the love that he had let go. Grimm informed Brahms that Agathe was still unmarried and had been going through difficult times. He could have taken the opportunity to connect with her, but he was more in the mood for self-pity than he was for action. He never even let Agathe know he was in town.

This period of romantic sentimentality brought forth some passionate songs and chamber music. One of the new pieces was his G Major Sextet, in which he spells out Agathe's name with the notes at the climax. Later in the piece, he uses the notes A, D, and E, signifying a farewell, to say goodbye to Agathe once and for all.

The G Major Sextet marked a change in Brahms's writing. It showed a depth of feeling that had not been present in his earlier compositions. He wrote out of his own longing and pain, and the message of heartache was something to which all people who had lost loves could relate.

From this point on Brahms's music strove for maturity. He began focusing more on what he wanted the audience to feel and less on his own emotions. He stopped writing word games into his melodies, and quit revealing so much of his personal life. The music became a mask for him, as would the beard he began growing and the weight he gained. Brahms had developed many ways to bury his feelings deep inside.

Chapter Five
A German Requiem

On February 2, 1865, Johannes Brahms's mother passed away at the age of seventy-six. His brother, Fritz, had sent him a letter about Christiane's failing health, and though Johannes rushed to Hamburg to be at his mother's side, he arrived a day too late. His mother's death gave thirty-one-year-old Brahms reason to pause and think about his own life.

By most people's standards, he was quite accomplished. But Brahms was not satisfied. He was not married and had no children. He had never written an opera or a symphony. With the exception of the D Minor Piano Concerto and a couple of serenades, all of his pieces were for small chamber groups, choruses, or solo piano. But something was brewing in his mind that he thought would prove his worth as a composer. He had been thinking about writing a requiem.

Brahms's mother Christiane in 1862. *(Courtesy of Kurt Hoffman, Hamburg.)*

Requiems were typically music written for a Catholic ceremony commemorating the dead. The texts were generally in Latin, the official language of the Catholic Church at that time. Brahms had been raised as a Protestant but was not particularly religious; he decided to write his requiem in German. His mother's death inspired him to complete the piece he had so far only envisioned. Writing this score would occupy most of his attention for an entire year.

Brahms spent the summer of 1865 in a small town called Lichtenstein, and it proved to be a perfect place for composing. Not only did he manage to finish most of *A German Requiem,* but he also wrote movements for a string sextet and the E Minor Cello Sonata, as well as a trio for piano, violin, and French horn. He played concerts, renewed old friendships with Julius Stockhausen and Theodore Kirchner, saw a performance of Bach's *St. Matthew Passion,* drank plenty of beer and coffee, and flirted with pretty singers whenever he had the chance. His beard continued growing, as did his belly.

He was in an agreeable mood that summer despite the death of his mother. Most of that good feeling stemmed from his musical pursuits. Brahms was estranged from his brother and sister due to the strain of recent family events. The only family member Brahms enjoyed seeing was his father. The two of them had become much closer over the past year. In October 1865, Johann Jakob wrote to his son that he was planning to get married again, this time to a younger woman named Karoline Shnack. Brahms, who had worked to keep his parents together, wrote cheerfully to his father: "Dearest Father, a thousand blessings and the warmest wishes for your well-being accompanying you from here. How gladly I would sit at your side, press your hand, and wish you as much happiness as you deserve, which would be more than enough for one earthly lifetime." Brahms genuinely liked Karoline, took to calling her "mother," and even helped take care of her ailing son (who Brahms nicknamed "the second Fritz" because he had the same name as Brahms's brother).

That same month, Levi conducted a performance of Brahms's D Minor Piano Concerto in the German city of Karlsruhe, and it was a great success. The concerto was finally finding an appreciative audience. To promote the piece, Brahms decided to make a tour of the German-speaking territories in northern Europe, which included the Netherlands, Denmark, Sweden, Switzerland, and Prussia. Mostly, he traveled by train or horse-drawn carriage. Roads were paved in the metropolitan areas, so although travel was time-consuming, it was not terribly difficult. Brahms would travel by boat up the many rivers of northern Europe, but only if he could see the shore at all times. He was afraid of open water.

This journey marked his first real tour as a solo pianist, and because his work was so well received, he forgot his usual distaste for the performing life. "I will tell you in detail," he gushed to Clara, "how successful I have been, as a matter of fact quite beyond expectation in every way. What has pleased me most is that I really have the gifts of a virtuoso." Clara probably found that statement quite amusing after his years of complaining about having to play concerts to earn money when he would rather be composing.

At Christmas, Brahms traveled to the court of Detmold to play concerts. While there, he had a letter from Clara saying her daughter Julie was sick with typhoid, so Brahms rushed to be with the family. His feelings for Julie were especially tender. She had grown into a beautiful nineteen-year-old woman, and he could not help but find himself attracted to her. At the same time, he had been something of a substitute father to her since Schumann died, so he knew that his romantic feelings for her were inappropriate.

He never shared these feelings with Clara, of course; given their history together, doing so would have put a great strain on their friendship. Still, Brahms took every chance to be near the girl, and showered her with special attention. Upon hearing that she suffered such a terrible illness, he made seeing her a priority over any of his musical endeav-

Robert and Clara Schumann's daughter Julie.

ors. He stayed with the family through the holidays, and though Julie's health did not improve much before he had to leave for his next concert date, his presence put everyone in better spirits.

In January 1866, Brahms's friend Albert Dietrich organized a "Brahms week" in Oldenburg—a weeklong festival of his works. Brahms stopped there to enjoy the adulation and another successful performance of his D Minor Piano Concerto before embarking on a tour of Switzerland. By this point, however, the joy of playing concerts had once again worn off. He no longer wanted to play piano; he wanted to finish writing *A German Requiem.*

For the summer of 1866, Brahms went back to Baden-Baden. He finished the requiem that August. Perhaps because he had finally finished his first substantial work, Brahms was in good spirits for the rest of the summer, spending much of his time with Clara and her children. Clara took note of the extra attention Brahms paid to Julie and did not approve, nor was she happy with the beard he had grown. Reluctantly, Brahms shaved it off, though at the time many sophisticated gentlemen wore beards.

The first person to whom Brahms showed *A German Requiem* was Clara, who had reservations about the repeated note in the work's final movement. She thought the repetition superfluous, and worried that it might ruin an otherwise outstanding piece of music. Stubborn as always, Brahms refused to change anything.

Soon after that summer, Brahms's mood began to sour again. It started with a concert in February of 1867, when his G Major Sextet was premiered in Vienna to terrible reviews. "This prophet proclaimed by Robert Schumann," the critic for Vienna's most important newspaper wrote, "is in his darkening hours." The critic also referred to the music as "products of the most desperate effort." Brahms continued to tour with Joachim, and seemed to put the bad reviews behind him, but then he heard more aggravating news. His friend Stockhausen had resigned from his post at the Hamburg Philharmonic, and once again the Philharmonic offered the position to someone else—someone eminently less qualified than the now-famous Brahms. On top of it all, Brahms was having trouble getting *A German Requiem* performed anywhere. It was too hard for amateur choruses, and no professional groups expressed any interest in it.

Frustrated, Brahms became more irritable than ever, insulting his friends and being generally difficult. Clara found his moody behavior insufferable, and cancelled invitations she had made to him for dinners at her home. Some aching and beautiful songs came out of his frustration, but he was too spent from composing his *Requiem* to even think of beginning another large-scale piece. He needed a break.

Brahms brought his father to Vienna for a visit. Johann Jakob had barely set foot outside of his own hometown, so the journey was quite an adventure. Brahms showed his father all the famous Viennese sights and took him to his favorite cafés and beer gardens. They climbed the 5,850-foot high Schafberg Mountain together, visited Mozart's birthplace in Salzburg, and even managed to catch a glimpse of the Austrian emperor, Franz Joseph, while touring the Schönbrünn Palace. Spending this time with his father rejuvenated Brahms's spirits, and he wrote to Joachim of the visit: "I experienced the greatest happiness I have felt in a long time. . . . My soul is refreshed like a body after a bath. My good father hasn't the slightest idea how much good he has done me." As his mood elevated, Brahms heard that some portions of his *Requiem* would finally be performed in Vienna, on December 1, 1867.

The first three movements of *A German Requiem* received very mixed reactions. Some loved it, some actively hated it, booing and hissing at the end in apparent agreement with Clara's initial negative assessment of the final movement. Hanslick wrote: "While the first two movements of the *Requiem,* in spite of their somber gravity, were received with unanimous applause, the fate of the third movement was very doubtful. . . . During the concluding fugue of the third movement . . . [one] experienced the sensations of a passenger rattling through a tunnel in an express train."

Brahms was certain that the music was not at fault. He felt the problem was with the under-rehearsed musicians, the conductor, and the man who played the timpani. The timpanist had perhaps not fully understood the third movement, and he had played his repeated note (the very one Clara had worried about) as loudly as possible, making the problematic note impossible to ignore. The *Requiem* would get another chance, though. Word came from the port city of Bremen that the premiere of the entire piece, with a proper three months of rehearsal, would take place there the following year.

In January 1868, Brahms went home to Hamburg to play some concerts, see his father, and, because Hamburg was very close to Bremen, keep an eye on rehearsals. He even consented to play a Beethoven piano concerto with the Hamburg Philharmonic, though they had now twice rejected him for the position of music director. He and Julius Stockhausen set out on a concert tour that would culminate in a number of performances in Copenhagen, Denmark. The tour was going well until, after one of the Copenhagen concerts, Brahms's

The title page for the first edition of Brahms's *German Requiem. (Courtesy of the British Library, London.)*

Another view of Brahms's Hamburg. His emotions for his hometown were complicated by his feeling that the city had repeatedly rejected him. *(Courtesy of Museum für Geschichte, Dresden.)*

crass behavior spoiled it. Brahms offended the Danish people by remarking at a party being held in his honor, to a roomful of Danish dignitaries and music lovers, that it was a shame a beloved Danish artist's works were displayed in Copenhagen, rather than in a sophisticated German city like Berlin. This comment insulted the entire country's pride. The remaining concerts were cancelled, angry articles immediately appeared in newspapers, and Brahms, seeming to take a perverse delight in the turmoil he caused, left for Hamburg refusing to apologize.

Clara wrote to Brahms that she would be unable to attend the premiere of *A German Requiem* due to a long tour she was about to undertake. Brahms came dangerously close to permanently damaging their friendship when he wrote her a letter that apparently intended to make her feel guilty for leaving her daughter Julie when she was so sick. Clara was furious, and wrote him "You really seem to be under the illusion that I have enough and am touring for my own entertainment. But surely one would not make all these exertions merely for pleasure!" She was outraged at his insinuation that she cared more for her piano playing than her children. Raising children alone had been difficult, to say the least, but she had always done her conscientious best.

Clara was also angry that although Brahms respected her as a musician, he never took her career as a performer very seriously. He could never understand why she loved playing the piano so much. She tried to explain it to him once. "You regard it only as a way to earn money," she wrote to him, "I do not. I feel a calling to reproduce great works, above all . . . the works of Robert, as long as I have the strength to do so. . . . The practice of art is, after all, the great part of my inner self. To me, it is the very air I breathe." Brahms backed down, apologizing, and once more a rift was mended.

As the premiere of *A German Requiem* neared, Brahms became very anxious. If he succeeded with his first big piece, he would have money and fame. Should he fail, he might never hear another of his orchestral pieces performed in his lifetime.

On April 10, 1868, a month before Brahms turned thirty-five, the cathedral in Bremen was packed for the performance. Some in the audience hoped for a success, and some for a fiasco. Among those present were important composers, critics, and performers. A large orchestra and a chorus

The Bremen Cathedral, site of Brahms's *German Requiem* triumph. *(Focke Museum, Bremen.)*

of over two hundred people filled the altar. Even Clara, despite her tour and the tension in their relationship, made a surprise appearance. Brahms was deeply touched by her presence and escorted her to a front-row seat. Then he took the stage, lifted his baton, and the orchestra began to play.

The concert went over tremendously well. After the performance, Brahms was surrounded by friends and showered with compliments. Karl Reinthaler, the director who had prepared the orchestra and chorus so carefully over the past three months, made a speech, saying, "What we have heard today is a great and beautiful work, deep and intense in feeling, ideal and lofty in conception. Yes, one may call it an epoch-making work!" Applause and cheers rang out all around and Clara cried as Brahms addressed the adoring crowd and thanked all the performers.

After such an overwhelming success, Brahms was drained. He went to his father's house in Hamburg to recuperate and to enjoy the quiet of his hometown. He hoped to walk along the familiar trails and visit friends and family. But word of Brahms's music had begun to spread, and people were clamoring for copies and performance rights. Brahms had become a success on his own terms: not as a pianist, playing other people's music, but as a composer. In the coming year there would be twenty performances of *A German Requiem* in Germany alone, and more in Russia, England, and France. Brahms had secured for himself an elevated place in the European musical community.

But, still, he was uneasy. Now that the music world depended on him to produce masterpieces, his fear of failure was stronger than ever. He had become all that Schumann had predicted, but worried that his fame would be fleeting. Brahms had yet to write a symphony, and this would be his most daunting challenge.

Chapter Six
From Sorrow to Symphony

At thirty-five years old, Johannes Brahms was a well-known and successful composer in firm control of his musical style and his career. If his music had already moved from romantic but immature writings to deeper, more passionate and mature pieces, his music from this point on would take on a stately, majestic cast, becoming less impetuous, more commanding and controlled.

Brahms continued to be compared to Beethoven and remained haunted by the comparison. He was no longer flattered to be spoken of in such terms. He wanted to be a great composer in his own right, but he had not yet tackled three very important compositional forms: the string quartet, the opera, and the symphony.

Brahms saw the symphony as the steepest hurdle he faced. Beethoven's symphonies had surpassed those of any composer before him. He had used Mozart's work as a jumping-off point, and then expanded the form to meet his own voracious needs. In some instances he had switched the order of the movements and in others he had made his own hybrid form, as in the case of the Ninth Symphony, when he added voices, something that had never been done before. Many composers since Beethoven had written symphonies, but none was considered his equal. Wagner said, famously, that Beethoven had taken the form to its highest possible level, and that after him the symphony was dead, a historical relic.

Despite his triumphs, Brahms felt like a failed man in some respects. "I'll never write a symphony!" he complained to Hermann Levi. About Beethoven, he continued, "You have no idea how the likes of us feel when we're always hearing a giant like that behind us."

Over the next few years Johannes Brahms established a routine for his daily life—a predictable and simple lifestyle that allowed him to save all his creative thought for his music. He awakened early each day to have a cup of coffee and smoke half a cigar before doing anything. Then he would get to work composing or studying the works of others. He filled the rest of his day with long walks, and always ate his lunches and dinners out with friends.

Like his days, the cycle of his years followed an established routine. Most of the year he lived in Vienna, but he always spent his summers composing in Baden-Baden or at other scenic getaways. In the early spring, Brahms could usually be found touring the German territories, promoting his music. He had come to enjoy traveling, especially now that he could afford to travel in the comfortable cabins of trains.

In 1868, in between scribbling down notes for the symphony he planned to write, Brahms wrote some of his most delightful songs. One was a lullaby called *Wiegenlied* (Cradle Song), originally written to celebrate the birth of a friend's child. Soon, this tune was the most well-known lullaby ever written. A wide variety of arrangements were published and distributed, which made a great deal of money for such a tiny piece of music. Brahms wrote to his publisher, Simrock, half in complaint and half in jest, "Why not make a new edition in a Minor key for naughty or sick children? That would be still another way to move copies."

That October, Brahms composed a set of pieces called

the *Liebeslieder (Love Song) Waltzes*. Clara adored them, completely unaware that this set was inspired by the composer's love for her daughter, Julie. The *Liebeslieder* and some of his Hungarian Dances (based on gypsy melodies) were published in November 1868, and Brahms suddenly found himself wealthy. His career was different from other great composers of earlier

Brahms's friend and publisher Fritz Simrock. Brahms's music eventually made Simrock a wealthy man. *(Courtesy of Kurt Hoffman, Hamburg.)*

generations in that he had never been hired by a rich noble to write a piece of music. He made enough money from the publication of his work (more than any other composer ever had before) to have complete creative freedom to write whatever he wished. Brahms's career marked the beginning of the end of the patronage system.

The following summer, Brahms learned that Julie, now twenty-three, was going to be married. Clara was upset because she did not believe her daughter's frail body could withstand a pregnancy. Brahms's sorrow lay in his realization that Julie would now be completely out of his reach. Although he had never told Clara that he loved her daughter, and had never made any romantic advances toward Julie, Brahms had fantasized about marrying her. She was one more in a list of woman he would love and never have. When the marriage was announced, Brahms ran out of the Schumanns' home in tears, for the first time revealing to Clara and Julie how he truly felt. Clara was shocked by this revelation, but their complicated friendship remained intact, able to weather yet another storm.

Soon after this incident, Brahms began one of his finest works, the *Alto Rhapsody*. A rhapsody is not technically a musical form like a sonata or concerto, rather, it is a Romantic expression used to describe intuitive music, which tends to be epic or heroic in nature. Brahms's dark, brooding piece is perfectly suited to its form. This work overflows with all of his life's heartaches. The G Major Sextet may have been a farewell to Agathe, but the *Alto Rhapsody* was a farewell to love altogether. He would never again write such an aching piece of music because he would never fall in love with another woman. He proclaimed himself to be a determined bachelor.

While he was writing the *Alto Rhapsody,* Julie was married. At the wedding Brahms feigned an amiable and sweet demeanor. A week later, he played the finished *Alto Rhapsody* for Clara, who loved it and understood that it was Brahms's lament for his lost bride. She wrote in her journal, "It is long since I remember being moved by a depth of pain in words and music. . . . this piece seems to me neither more nor less than the expression of his own heart's anguish. If only he would for once speak as tenderly!"

Brahms fell into another depression, and 1870 started out on a poor note. Even the Vienna premiere of the *Liebeslieder Waltzes,* with Brahms and Clara at the keyboards, did little to lift his spirits.

One piece of bad news followed on the heels of another. He learned that his father was ill and had pain in his hands and feet that forced him to resign his position as a bass player in the Hamburg Philharmonic. His sister, Elise, announced that she was going to marry a sixty-year-old man with six children. Brahms was against the idea because he feared that taking care of all those children would worsen her already bad health. He urged her to enter the convent instead. Elise ignored him, married, and ultimately proved her brother's fears unfounded.

His friends could not offer any consolation. Joachim was having difficulty with his marriage, and Clara's life was in turmoil. Her career was threatened by pain in her hands and failing hearing, and her son, Ludwig, had been pronounced insane and sent to an asylum, like his father. Her youngest boy, Brahms's godson Felix, was sick with tuberculosis, and Ferdinand, another of her sons, had just enlisted in the Prussian army. The misery mounted steadily, and Brahms's depression grew.

The Prime Minister of Prussia, Otto von Bismarck, started a war with France to seize territory and to unify Germany under Prussian leadership. The area we now think of as Germany had been a region of loosely affiliated states until Bismarck acted to bring them together. The war lasted two years—Prussia defeated the French in 1871. The war made life in Germany difficult: every German was terrified of the sounds of cannons blasting and the threat of invasion by the French.

All the railways were reserved for the military, so Brahms could not go to comfort Clara in Baden-Baden. Trapped in Vienna, he used his time to compose a patriotic work that hoped for Prussian victory and peace thereafter—the *Triumphlied* (Song of Triumph). This music, written for two four-part choirs and a full orchestra, was the best Brahms could do for the war effort.

Germany was unified under one flag in January 1871, as Karl Wilhelm I was pronounced *Kaiser* of the German Empire. Brahms's *Triumphlied* was a rousing success throughout much of Europe, except, understandably, in France.

In 1871, Brahms, now thirty-eight years old, beardless but increasingly round in the middle, gave up living out of

Brahms's Vienna apartment, where the watchful bust of Beethoven looked down on Brahms's work.

hotel rooms and took up permanent residence in Vienna. He decorated his third-floor apartment with only a few simple pieces of furniture; his piano, which had belonged to Robert Schumann; and the bust of Beethoven. Nothing about his home reflected the large sums of money he earned from his music except for his collections of music manuscripts, books, and tin soldiers. He lived frugally, shopping for bargains whenever possible.

Brahms was offered a position as the music director for the Gesellschraft der Musikfreunde. This was the top job in the city, especially now that the Gesellschraft orchestra had moved into a brand new theater. With a huge orchestra and chorus at his disposal, he could try out his new pieces and conduct favorite works by Bach and Schumann. Brahms accepted the post with enthusiasm.

Shortly after beginning his work with the Gesellschraft, however, Brahms received news that sent him back to Hamburg—his father was dying of liver cancer. Brahms was with him at the end, though neither of his siblings came to their father's bedside. After the funeral, Brahms left Hamburg for good, though he did continue to send money to his family members, including his stepmother and her son.

He returned to Vienna ready to focus all of his energy on rehearsals for the upcoming performance with the Gesellschraft orchestra. He demanded that the three-hundred-member choir increase their rehearsals from one a week to two. He was not considered an overly strict master though, and was known for his wit. One of his favorite jokes was to say, "I'm in a really good mood today so let's do *Dear Lord When Shall I Die?*" His conducting was disorganized but passionate.

November 10, 1872 marked Brahms's first performance with one of the grandest orchestras in all of Europe and should have been a crowning moment in his life. But his memory of that night would always be tainted by the tragedy that occurred the very same day. Clara's fears were realized when her frail daughter, Julie, died giving birth.

Clara decided not go to Baden-Baden the following summer. She was grieving and wanted to stay at her home in Berlin where she could better care for Felix, who was still sick with tuberculosis. With their usual summer plans cancelled, Brahms decided to spend the summer of 1873 in a village called Grätwein. There, on a rickety, broken-down piano he rented, the clean air and beautiful weather inspired Brahms to write the *Haydn Variations,* his first set of variations in over ten years. This piece began as a composition for two pianos—the largest keyboard work of his life. Later, under Levi's influence, he arranged the *Haydn Variations* for full symphony orchestra.

The piece is based on a simple chorale tune of Franz Joseph Haydn's, an Austrian composer of the Classical period. Brahms makes his own music out of the tune, though, with a sprawling set of variations. Haydn's melody is almost buried under the weight of Brahms's inventions, and when it finally emerges in the last variation it does so triumphantly.

Brahms finished the *Haydn Variations* as he turned forty and immediately set to work on another challenge, attempting to master the string quartet (music written for two violins, viola, and cello). Mozart and Haydn had both written hundreds of these, and some of Beethoven's most sublime music can be found in the sixteen he composed. Very few composers had dared attempt a string quartet since Beethoven's death, and those who had merely dabbled in the form.

Brahms discarded twenty attempts before finishing the String Quartets in C Minor and A Minor (Opus 51). He turned the string quartet form, as developed by Haydn and Mozart, inside out. Contemporary listeners were confused by his work, and today these two pieces remain among his least popular.

Franz Joseph Haydn, whose compositions inspired Brahms.

In 1873, the Vienna stock exchange collapsed and Austria fell into an economic depression. Nearly all of the banks involved in the crash were owned and operated by Jewish bankers so, in keeping with the anti-Semitic sentiment on the rise in much of Europe, the Jews were blamed for the disaster. Anti-Semitism escalated, particularly in Austria and Germany, and would continue to do so well into the next century.

Everyone in Austria suffered during the depression. Brahms's income went down as fewer people attended concerts or bought sheet music to play at home. In the midst of this tough financial period, Brahms premiered his two string quartets and led the Vienna Philharmonic in the first performance of the *Haydn Variations*. The *Variations* were a hit, and the response encouraged Brahms to continue composing pieces for orchestra.

His fame was spreading beyond the city limits of Vienna and across Europe. Cambridge University in England wanted to give Brahms an honorary doctorate, but because he was afraid to sail across the English Channel to accept the honor personally, the offer was withdrawn. King Ludwig II of Bavaria knighted him, though Brahms would never let anyone call him by his new title. Wagner was also offered a knighthood by King Ludwig but was so angry that Brahms had received his first, he threatened to decline the honor.

After three seasons and eighteen concerts with the Gesellschraft, Brahms resigned his conductorship in February 1875, saying he needed more time to compose. He decided to spend a summer near the city of Heidelberg, where he rented a small cottage. There, he worked on a piano quartet (a piece for piano and three string instruments) and composed another string quartet, this one in the key of B-flat Major. At the end of the summer, he took time to travel. He had still not begun a symphony.

Returning to Vienna in June 1876, Brahms knew he had procrastinated. He wrote to a friend, "from time to time I write highly useless pieces in order not to have to look into the stern face of a symphony." He was clearly nervous about taking on such a major work. Brahms's fame was such that critics and music enthusiasts alike would closely examine any composition he produced, and he feared the possibility that his work would be found lacking. After his years with the Gesellschraft and his companionship with Levi, he finally felt he had enough experience with a full orchestra to know how to proceed. Under the bust of Beethoven, Brahms finally started working on a symphony.

Three months later, in August 1876, Brahms drew the final double bar at the end of his C Minor Symphony. A heavy, ponderous work, teeming with Beethoven's spirit, the symphony even makes veiled reference to the "Ode to Joy" tune from Beethoven's Ninth Symphony. When Brahms's symphony premiered, admirers quickly dubbed it Beethoven's Tenth. A success then, the work is still hailed as a masterpiece today. At long last, Brahms had lived up to all that the music world expected of him. The public hailed him as a worthy heir to Beethoven's crown, but Brahms was not one to rest on his laurels. There was much more work to be done.

Over: A section from Edgar Degas's painting *Orchestra at the Opera. (Courtesy of Bildarchiv der Oesterreichischen National bibliothek, Vienna.)*

Chapter Seven
Working Summers

Completing his First Symphony did not change Brahms's yearly schedule. He continued touring primarily during the winter seasons, with the sole purpose of giving his music more exposure. He still did most of his composing during the summer months at a retreat in the country or the mountains. The next decade of summers would be the most prolific of his life.

Brahms spent the summer after writing the First Symphony writing his Second. Both Beethoven and Schubert had written nine symphonies; Robert Schumann wrote four; Brahms, with only one, had a lot of catching up to do. At a village called Pörtshach on Lake Worth he composed his Second Symphony, finishing the entire piece in only four months.

Written in D Major, the Second Symphony is joyous and

full of lively tunes, as opposed to the more somber sound of the C Minor Symphony. This new piece looked back to happier times, even beginning with a waltz. Many people compared it to Beethoven's Sixth Symphony. Known as the Pastoral, it is the lightest and happiest piece Beethoven ever wrote.

When the Second Symphony was performed in Vienna in December 1877, exactly one year after the First Symphony had been premiered, one critic wrote, "That symphony is like blue heavens, the murmur of springs, sunshine and cool green shadows!" Brahms's old friend, the critic Eduard Hanslick, called it an "Unqualified Success."

The following April, Brahms took a vacation to Italy, the only country he ever traveled to that did not have German as its primary language. He enjoyed visiting Italian cities, and soaked up the food, wine, and art. But he was not as impressed by their musical culture. While away from home, he finally grew out his beard, and when he re-

A contemporary caricature of a stout Brahms, alluding to his fondness for the Viennese restaurant The Red Hedgehog. *(Courtesy of Gesellschaft der Musikfreunde, Vienna.)*

Joseph Joachim, Brahms's longtime friend and performing partner. *(Courtesy of Mansell Collection.)*

turned to Vienna he had a great time hiding behind it, fooling people who did not recognize him. Between 1878 and 1893 Brahms would spend eight more springs in Italy.

Lake Worth had proven to be a great place for composing, so Brahms returned for another summer, this time to write a violin concerto. This project thrilled Joachim, who longed to have a new, important showpiece for his violin skills. The two friends began a flurry of correspondence, and Brahms made good use of Joachim's violin expertise. Joachim pressured Brahms to finish quickly, for he had arranged to play the concerto in Leipzig on New Year's Day, just months away. This commitment did not, however, stop Brahms from taking time to compose songs and piano pieces when the mood struck him. During this time he also traveled to Hamburg, a podium that represented dual failures to the sensitive Brahms, to guest conduct his Second Symphony.

When Joachim played the Violin Concerto in front of the ever-difficult Leipzig audience their reaction was cool, but this was to be expected in a town that still gave its allegiance to the New German School and thought Brahms's music old-fashioned. The work itself is full of beautiful tunes, but they come late in the piece, which forces the audience to be patient. In the slow movement, the work's most poignant melody is given to the oboe, a fact that irritates violin aficionados to this day.

After the Vienna premiere of the Violin Concerto in January 1879, Felix Schumann died of tuberculosis. Brahms rushed to comfort Clara through another difficult time. She was fifty-nine years old when she lost her son, and the years of worry and strain had worn their way into her features. Pain in her arm made it nearly impossible for her to play, and her hearing had worsened considerably.

Later that year, a monument to Robert Schumann was unveiled at his gravesite in Bonn. Because Clara could not play the piano for the ceremony, Brahms was asked to play Robert Schumann's E-flat Major Piano Quartet. Though it was indeed an honor to have Brahms playing her husband's music, his keyboard skills had degraded so much that it pained Clara to hear him botch his way through it. She wrote in her journal, "I felt as if I were sitting on thorns, and so did Joachim, who kept casting despairing glances at me."

As the 1870s gave way to the 1880s, Brahms opted for a change of scenery and spent his summer in Bad Ischl, just outside of Salzburg. He began two trios for piano, cello, and violin. He also wrote a choral piece, began a second piano concerto, and completed two orchestral pieces, which were not really symphonies in his opinion, so he chose to call them overtures. The term overture usually refers to the piece of instrumental music that begins an opera, but Brahms felt the title suited his works anyway.

In the meantime, Joachim was still having marital problems. He was certain that his wife, Amalie, was cheating on him. Brahms believed otherwise, and wrote to her expressing his faith. He had no way of knowing that four years later this letter

Franz Liszt's son-in-law and Richard Wagner's close friend, Hans von Bülow defied convention by also admiring Brahms.

would be used as a defense of her character in the couple's divorce hearings. It seemed to Joachim that Brahms had taken Amalie's side in the matter. Years went by before Joachim would speak to Brahms, and their friendship would never fully recover.

For the next two summers Brahms concentrated on chamber music. He completed his second piano concerto, which was previewed that autumn by Hans von Bülow, one of the rare musicians of the age who was devoted to both Wagner and Brahms. Bülow set out to prove that one could love both masters, even if the masters themselves did not particularly care for each other's work. In July of 1882, Bülow invited Brahms to see the world premiere of Wagner's opera *Parsifal*. Brahms declined, having learned that his friend Levi was conducting the opera and was meanwhile suffering all sorts of anti-Semitic treatment from Wagner.

Levi, so enamored of Wagner's talent, forgave the slights from the composer about his Jewish heritage, but Brahms was offended. Anti-Semitism had become a rampant problem in Austria, and Brahms, who had many Jewish friends, could not see how this hatred could be good for the country. "I can scarcely speak of it, it seems so despicable to me," he told a friend about the way Jews were being treated. For this reason, he refused to support Wagner's work any longer, and he had difficulty respecting Levi's position.

Richard Wagner died that winter. Brahms heard the news during a rehearsal for one of his own choral works. Despite years of rivalry, battles of opinion, and thousands of bitter words, he stopped rehearsal and said, "Today we sing no more. A master has died." He sent sincere condolences to Wagner's family.

On May 7, 1883, Brahms gathered his bachelor friends around him and celebrated his fiftieth birthday, laughing and drinking the night away. Earlier that year, he had met a beautiful young singer, Hermine Spies. She introduced herself by singing one of his more risqué love songs, and they began a flirtation that carried on for years. Brahms spent the summer of 1883 in Weisbaden because Hermine was also staying there. He let her lovely voice inspire him to produce reams of *lieder*, though most of these songs were

Even in his old age, Brahms enjoyed the company of attractive young women. Though he flirted, he never married. *(Courtesy of Bildarchiv der Oesterreichischen National bibliothek.)*

anything but happy. He wrote about the frustration of aging, and, of course, about regret. A line from one of his songs in Opus 94 reads, "No house, no homeland, no wife and no child; thus I am whirled like a straw in storm and wind!" In between these sad songs, Brahms finished his Third Symphony.

When the Third Symphony was played for the first time, in Vienna on December 2, 1883, it received strong reactions. Avid fans of Wagner went to the event just to boo and hiss at the composer, but more enthusiastic fans of Brahms soon silenced them. Critics called the Third Symphony the best that Brahms had ever written. For the first time since *A German Requiem,* he had a huge hit. Orchestras everywhere sought out copies of the symphony and pressed Brahms to come conduct, or at least to grace their audiences with his presence.

The accolades and standing ovations were flattering, but they also gave Brahms reason to worry. He wondered if people were really impressed with his music or just by his celebrity. Also troubling the moody composer were the number of permanent conducting jobs he was offered. He turned them all down but could not help wondering why his hometown of Hamburg still had not offered him a position with their Philharmonic. This perceived ongoing slight nagged at Brahms to no end.

Vienna, however, was one city completely won over by Brahms. As president of a newly formed musicians' club, he spent Monday nights with local celebrities, telling jokes, eating good food, and drinking beer and coffee. He began to take young composers under his wing, looking at their music and offering advice—perhaps remembering the sting of Robert Schumann's initial rebuff so many years ago. Still, Brahms was not an easy mentor and his criticism could be sharp.

In the summer of 1885, Brahms continued to write vocal music but also completed his fourth and final symphony. Anxious for his friends to hear it, he gathered them one evening at a Vienna bar and played through it on the bar's clunky piano. Their response was not encouraging. They were unsure what to make of this strange new work. The opening melody struck them as more of a loose idea than a discernible tune, and at one moment the music broke into a sort of mad German tango. His friends suggested that he rewrite most of the symphony before playing it for anyone else.

His friends were, apparently, wrong in their judgment. Brahms did not change a note, and the October 1885 performance in Meiningen of his Fourth Symphony was met with a wild ovation. In city after city the symphony was a triumph. The Viennese premiere was greeted mildly, with the local critic writing that it was a good symphony but not as good as his last one, but Brahms believed it the finest of the four.

The summer of 1886 was his most productive yet, but it would also be the last one that was truly prolific. He wrote a cello sonata, two violin sonatas, a piano trio, and more *lieder*. Franz Liszt, the piano virtuoso who had given Brahms so many headaches, passed away that July. As with Wagner, Brahms could not help but feel a certain respect for his rival, and he said of Liszt, "Whoever has not heard Liszt cannot even speak of piano playing. He comes first and then for a long space nobody follows." Eduard Marxsen, Brahms's old piano teacher, died during this time as well.

Brahms became increasingly aware of his own mortality, and he turned his attention from creating new music to forming the legacy by which he wished to be remembered. Always conscious of the power of history, Brahms set about shaping his own.

Chapter Eight
Farewell

Biographers were showing great interest in writing Johannes Brahms's story, and he hated the idea. He wrote to Clara Schumann, asking her to send back all of the letters he had written to her over the years. He, in turn, promised to return all of hers. Brahms feared biographers would put his personal life on display. His plan was to burn everything before they could get to it.

Clara agreed to do this for him, but she took her time rereading all of his letters first. Apparently she also copied a few of her favorites or kept a few out of the box she returned to Brahms, for some of the letters survived Brahms's stove and did eventually find their way into print. More would have survived if Clara had been in lighter spirits. She had recently buried two children, and her son Ferdinand had become addicted to morphine after being injured in battle.

She wrote in her diary, "I had wanted to extract from [the letters] everything concerning his life as an artist and a human being, because they provide a more comprehensive portrait of him and his work than any biographer could possibly hope for . . . but he was adamant, and tearfully I let him have them today."

Along with the letters, Brahms burned the old manuscripts and unfinished scores he thought unworthy of his legacy. Fritz Simrock offered to republish many of Brahms's early piano pieces that had gone out of print. With a shrug, Brahms told Simrock to do so if he wished to, adding that before long the pieces would be worthless. Simrock did republish the music and Brahms asked him to put all of the proceeds into a special bank account. Brahms never touched a cent of it, and his will stated that the contents of the account should go entirely to the publisher. With this inheritance, Simrock would instantly be made a wealthy man.

After spending the summer of 1888 in Switzerland, producing songs and a violin sonata, Brahms returned to Vienna, anxious as always to show his newest music to Clara. Brahms organized a concert to celebrate the lengthy performing careers of both Clara and Joachim. Clara approached the stage to accept her applause but could only play a few measures before relinquishing the piano to another player. The pain in her arms was too great.

In December 1889, Brahms took the time to make one of the first voice recordings. The young inventor Thomas Edison asked him to record himself on his new machine, both speaking and playing the piano. Though it is garbled and hard to make out, Brahms introduces himself in his high, squeaky voice, and bangs out a bit of one of his Hungarian Dances.

The G Major String Quintet, which received rave reviews when it was first performed, would be Brahms's cheery farewell to music. He wrote to a friend: "My whole life I've been a hard worker; now for once I'm going to be good and lazy." Once, at a party, he heard someone playing rag-

The American inventor Thomas Edison. Though he had limited formal education, his brilliant ideas forever altered the technology of communication. *(Courtesy of the Science Museum, London.)*

time music on a banjo, and his fingers itched to fiddle with the new American sounds, but then he sighed, saying that he was just too old to start learning anything new.

Old habits are not so easily broken, though, and Brahms could not be lazy even when he tried. In Vienna, he heard a concert featuring the clarinet (a single-reed woodwind instrument that came into use in the mid-1700s, mainly in France and England). Austrian and German orchestras did not often feature this instrument, and Mozart, who had loved the sound and wrote a famous clarinet concerto, once bemoaned that fact, saying, "Oh if only we had clarinets; you can't guess the lordly effect of symphony with flutes, oboes and clarinets." Brahms fell in love with the instrument, and he immediately set about writing two new works for it in the summer of 1891.

Brahms's resistance to biographers was so great that he actually threw one out of his house, accusing him of eavesdropping on his composing. Brahms was moody and sad. Elisabet von Stockhausen, his friend and former love, and his sister, Elise, had died within a few weeks of each other. Then, in 1893, the beautiful singer Hermine Spies died. Brahms became more irascible than ever. He went to parties, but when asked, as he often was, to play the piano, he would scowl, oblige for a few moments, and then storm away in a huff. He was both restless and tired.

In February 1894, two more of his good friends died. He felt his solitude in the world more than ever before, writing in despair, "Apart from Frau Schumann I'm not attached to anybody with my whole soul!" He regretted that he had never married or had children, convinced by this point that "true immortality lies in one's children."

During this time of sadness, Brahms had surprising news. The Hamburg Philharmonic finally offered him the post of music director. Brahms had spent much of his life openly lobbying for the job. It represented the respect of his hometown, a place where he had felt slighted for most of his career. When told the position was finally his, Brahms confounded everyone by declining. He used the offer as a chance to tell them what a mistake they had made by not hiring him years before.

Brahms continued to receive awards and degrees from all over Europe, and major cities everywhere wanted to host

Johannes Brahms in 1894. *(Photograph by Maria Fellinger, courtesy of Gesellschaft der Musikfreunde, Vienna.)*

festivals in his honor. His presence was requested everywhere, and his entrance compelled the attention of everyone in the room. He was besieged by requests to sit for paintings and photographs, to look at manuscripts, to come to dinner, to compose, to conduct, to simply write his name. Brahms treated the attention the way he treated almost everything else—he was alternately attracted and repelled by it.

The gaps of time between compositions became longer now. Brahms composed nothing in 1895. In that entire year he only managed to spend one day with Clara Schumann. They were both in good spirits as Brahms played some of his music for her. The two friends had seen so much of life together, and had finally put their petty quarrels and bickering aside. Now, in the twilight of their lives, Brahms played gentle tunes to amuse the woman he had loved for such a long time.

Several months later, Clara suffered a stroke. Brahms wrote to Clara's daughter, Marie, "if you think the worst is expected . . . let me know, so that I may come while those dear eyes are still open; for when they close so much will end for me." She did not insist Brahms come to visit, for Clara, though bedridden, seemed to be recovering.

The news of Clara's illness sent Brahms back to the keyboard. The piece, his last, is a series of four laments about death for low voice and piano, called *Four Serious Songs*. The lyrics for these songs came from the book of Ecclesiastes of the Bible. Brahms chose these particular verses to represent his feelings about the power of love, rather than as religious statements, and he thought of Clara as he wrote. Clara would not recover from her stroke, and Brahms would never see her alive again.

As he was writing *Four Serious Songs,* Brahms received the news, in May of 1896, that Clara had died. The last music she had heard was that of her long-dead husband, Robert, and she was buried beside him. Instead of joining in the procession at her funeral, Brahms sat with a friend and wept. Later, when he was able, he wrote to Joachim about this woman who was his first love and most faithful friend: "Will not our faces light up with joy whenever we think of her— of this glorious woman, whose presence we were privileged to enjoy for a long lifetime—with ever increasing admiration? Only in this way can we mourn her." He never heard *Four Serious Songs* performed. He could not bear to.

After Clara's death, Brahms's own health took a turn for the worse. Friends commented on how sick he looked. His skin had developed an odd sallow color and his limbs grew skinnier as his belly expanded. In those days, having a belly was a sign of prosperity and health, and Brahms had rarely been sick a day in his life. It was several months before he could be convinced to go to a spa in Karlsbad for treatment. Brahms gave the doctors strict orders not to tell him if the news was bad, so they merely told him he had jaundice, a condition related to liver malfunction that causes the skin to yellow. He did have jaundice, but he was also dying from cancer of the liver.

Brahms returned to Vienna, convinced his health was of no concern. He did not immediately notice his weight dropping because his maid secretly altered his clothes at

Brahms, near the end of his life. The yellowing of his eyes from his illness is nearly visible even in this black and white photograph.

night. Those around him saw the truth, though, as his skin went from yellow to almost green, his hair became stringy, and he became tremendously weak.

His entire life, he had made his friends into a kind of family. Now, he needed them more than ever. When he could no longer take his walks, they brought carriages around so he could get outdoors. He still joked, drank more wine than

This caricature of Brahms conducting provides a good idea of the composer's presence and personality. A gentle bear of a man, his love for music shaped his life. *(Courtesy of Oesterreichischen National bibliothek, Vienna.)*

he should have, and continued to attend musical events in Vienna as long as he could manage. Seldom did he touch the piano anymore, but he spent many quiet hours at his desk, a score of Bach's music propped up next to him.

The last time he heard his own music was in March 1897, when the Vienna Philharmonic played the Fourth Symphony. Afterwards, the ovation went on for almost an hour. Brahms had long struggled to find love on his own terms. Here was the love and admiration of thousands of strangers, offered to him with no hesitation or reservation. For most of his life, Brahms had held so much of himself back, only fully expressing himself in his music. This was his thanks. He stood to receive it, tears pouring down his face.

On the morning of April 3, 1897, Brahms's maid came into the room. He sat up as if to say something, then fell back to the pillow and never stirred again.

Three days later, Vienna's streets overflowed with mourners. The funeral procession traveled across the river Wien to the Musikverein, where Brahms had spent much of his life. His song "Farewell" was sung, and he was buried in a grave of honor in the Central Cemetery, his coffin carried by his closest surviving friends. Johannes Brahms's grave lies in the hallowed ground reserved for those composers who contributed so much to music that they changed it forever.

Brahms may have worried that he would be remembered only as a cranky perfectionist unable to love anyone who could love him back, but, as he hoped, his music is what is remembered best. His tender lullaby, intricate violin concertos, playful variations, and majestic symphonies reveal a lively, dedicated musician, who gave his life to his greatest love.

Timeline

1833   Johannes Brahms is born in Hamburg, Germany, on May 7.

1843   Brahms gives his first public piano recital; begins piano lessons with Eduard Marxsen; begins touring as a child prodigy.

1847   Is hired to teach piano to Adolph Giesemann's daughter in Winsen-an-der-Luhe.

1847- Composes his first sonatas; in 1852, departs on a concert
1852   tour with his friend, the violinist, Eduard Reményi.

1853   Brahms meets Joseph Joachim and Franz Liszt; on October 1, meets Robert Schumann; Breitkopt & Härtel publish some of Brahms's music.

1854   Robert Schumann is put in an asylum; Brahms comes to live with Clara and her children.

1856   Robert Schumann dies in July.

1857   Brahms completes his D Minor Concerto; becomes choirmaster and music teacher at court of Detmold.

1861   Moves to Vienna.

1862   Composes the *Paganini Variations.*

1863   Meets composer Richard Wagner; Brahms becomes conductor of Singakademie in Vienna for one season.

1864   Composes G Major Sextet.

1865   Brahms's mother dies on February 2; Brahms composes *A German Requiem.*

1866   The Austro-Prussian War breaks out, lasting for six weeks between June and August.

1868   Brahms composes the "Cradle Song," also known as *Brahms's Lullaby;* composes *Liebeslieder Waltzes* and *Hungarian Dances.*

1869   Composes *Alto Rhapsody.*

1871   Composes *Triumphlied* in celebration of King Karl Wilhelm I's becoming *Kaiser* of the German Empire; Brahms accepts post as conductor for Gesellschraft der Musikfreunde.

1873   Composes *Haydn Variations.*

1876   Completes his C Minor Symphony (First Symphony).

1877   Composes Second Symphony.

1879   Joachim premieres Brahms's Violin Concerto in Vienna.

1883   Brahms composes Third Symphony.

1885   Completes Fourth Symphony.

1886   Franz Liszt dies in July.

1889   Brahms makes a recording for Thomas Edison in December.

1896   Brahms composes *Four Serious Songs;* Clara Schumann dies in May.

1897   Johannes Brahms dies on April 3.

Glossary of Musical Terms

a cappella Performed by voices without instrumental accompaniment.

accompanist One who plays piano to support another instrumentalist or vocalist.

allemande A sixteenth-century dance in 2/2 time.

amateur From the word "lover," refers to a person who pursues something out of love for it rather than as a profession. People in amateur choruses or orchestras did not make a living playing music.

Baroque era A period in history that dates roughly from 1600 to 1750. The most famous composers from this era are Bach, Vivaldi, and Handel.

bass The largest member of the violin family with the deepest voice, the bass (or double bass, as it is called) has four thick strings that produce its characteristic low, rich sound.

cantata A religious play without scenery or staging that is sung by a choir.

chamber music Small works, one instrument on a part, usually played in a small room rather than a big concert hall.

choir or chorus A group of singers who perform choral compositions.

Classical period A period in history that dates roughly from

1750 to 1830. The most famous composers from this era are Mozart, Haydn, and Beethoven.

composition A piece of music written down for others to play.

concerto A piece of instrumental music which highlights a particular instrument.

conductor The director of a musical ensemble.

double-bar A mark of two vertical lines on the score, indicating the end of one section and the beginning of another. Heavily drawn lines signify the end of the entire piece.

fantasy An expressive musical form that allows the composer to write freely, following his imagination rather than a particular form.

harpsichord A keyboard instrument in which the strings are plucked by quills, as opposed to the piano, whose sound is produced when hammers strike the strings.

intermezzo A short piece, usually played between movements.

lieder The German word for songs (lied = song). Lieder of the Romantic era are typically expressive pieces written for piano and voice.

Mass The central service of the Roman Catholic Church.

meter A measure of time; the grouping of notes into patterns that form the music's pulse or beat. At the beginning of a piece, the meter is noted with a time signature (one number on top of another, similar in appearance to a fraction), where the top number states the number of beats per measure and the bottom number names the note that receives one full beat.

minuet A stately seventeenth-century dance in 3/4 time.

opera Originating in seventeenth-century Italy, a story set to music, usually entirely sung. Music, drama, scenery, costumes, dance, and other theatrical elements combine to make the art form complete.

orchestra A group of instruments divided into wind, brass, percussion, and string sections.

overture The introductory music at the beginning of an opera or musical; also, an independent composition written for an orchestra.

pastoral A piece that portrays or expresses aspects of rural, country life, especially in a romanticized way.

perfect pitch The ability to sing or recognize notes exactly, without the assistance of an instrument for reference.

polka A lively dance in 2/4 time; polkas originated in Eastern Europe and were widely popular in the 1800s.

premiere The first performance of a new piece of music.

prodigy A child possessing amazing talent.

protégé A particular teacher's star pupil.

quartet A piece of music written for four instruments; also, the group of four musicians that plays this music.

quintet A piece of music for five instruments; also, the group of five musicians that performs this music.

repertoire The list of pieces a certain group or soloist knows how to play.

requiem A Catholic Mass commemorating the dead.

rhapsody A musical form that is more intuitive and expressive than structured.

Romantic era A period in history dating roughly from 1830 to 1900. Some of the most famous composers from this era were Brahms, Schumann, and Wagner.

scherzo A fast, frenzied (or lively and playful) dance in triple time (3/4 or 6/8).

serenade Instrumental music combining elements of chamber and symphonic music and generally played outdoors in the evenings or at social events.

sextet A piece of music for six players; also the group of six musicians that performs these pieces.

sonata A composition for a solo or accompanied instrument, usually in three or four movements of varying tempo.

string quartet A piece of music scored for two violins, viola, and cello; also, the ensemble of four musicians that plays these pieces.

suite A musical work consisting of a set of a number of dances.

symphony A large-scale piece, usually in three or four movements, similar in many ways to a sonata but scored for full orchestra. The symphony has gone through great changes since its earlier Classical models, and the Romantic era saw developments in terms of the number and length of movements, number and variety of instruments, and dynamic and expressive range.

timpani Large percussion instruments for orchestras. Also called kettledrums.

trio A piece of music for three instruments; also, the group of musicians that performs these pieces.

venue A location for a performance or gathering.

virtuoso An expert performer on a particular instrument.

waltz A popular dance in 3/4 time.

Sources

CHAPTER ONE: Boyhood in Hamburg

p. 17, "as much as you know…" Jan Swafford, *Johannes Brahms: A Biography* (New York: Alfred A. Knopf, 1997), 20.

p. 21, "exhibited a rare acuteness of mind…" Ibid., 25.

p. 23, "These half-clad girls, to make…" Victor Seroff, *Men Who Made Musical History* (New York: Funk & Wagnalls, 1969), 148.

p. 27, "a little virtuoso called J. Brahms…" Swafford, *Johannes Brahms*, 47.

CHAPTER TWO: The Whirlwind Tour

p. 34, "His playing shows that…" Hans Gal, *Johannes Brahms: His Work and Personality* (London: Weidenfeld and Nicolson, 1963), 5.

p. 38, "If you get every little thing…" Swafford, *Johannes Brahms,* 71.

p. 38, "Allow me… to write and tell you…" Ibid., 71.

p. 41, "Visit from Brahms (a genius)." Ibid., 77.

p. 41, "Here again is one who comes…" Ibid., 77.

p. 45, "I thought that…" Gal, *Johannes Brahms,* 6-7.

p. 46, "You have made me so…" Swafford, *Johannes Brahms,* 88.

p. 46, "It really seems to me immaterial…" Jonathon Brown, *Johannes Brahms: An Essential Guide to his Life and Works* (London: Pavilion Books Ltd.,1996), 29.

p. 48, "someday become what Schumann…" Swafford, *Johannes Brahms,* 93.

CHAPTER THREE: Love in D Minor

p. 50, "That good Brahms…" Swafford, *Johannes Brahms,* 110.

p. 52, "I lose myself in it…" Ibid., 110.

p. 54, "I believe that I do not respect…" Hans Gal, *Johannes Brahms,* 90.

p. 56, "Thank you… my dear…" Swafford, *Johannes Brahms,* 127.

p. 55, "To me Schumann's memory is holy…" Gal, *Johannes Brahms,* 10.

p. 62, "Why shouldn't we two intelligent…" Ibid., 63.

p. 65, "new works do not succeed…" Swafford, *Johannes Brahms,* 190.

p. 65, "The failure has made no impression…" Ibid., 190.

p. 65, "if… I had had to meet the anxious…" Ibid., 191.

p. 66, "My fingers often itch…" Gal, *Johannes Brahms,* 35.

p. 68, "Every New Year…" Brown, *Johannes Brahms,* 48.

CHAPTER FOUR: City of Dreams

p. 72, "Yes, so it goes!…" Styra Avins, ed. *Johannes Brahms: Life and Letters* (Oxford: Oxford University Press, 1997), 248.

p. 75, "I had a devil of a time…" Swafford, *Johannes Brahms,* 265.

p. 76, "One sees what may still be done…" Ibid., 267.

p. 76, "lucky fellow…cradle" Brown, *Johannes Brahms,* 61.

p. 77, "How seldom does someone like us…" Avins, *Johannes Brahms,* 258.

p. 79, "that your choice as conductor…" Ibid., 280-281.

p. 80, "a very pretty girl…" Swafford, *Johannes Brahms,* 279.

CHAPTER FIVE: A German Requiem

p. 88, "Dearest Father, a thousand blessings…" Swafford, *Johannes Brahms,* 301.

p. 89, "I will tell you in detail…" Ibid., 304.

p. 91, "This prophet proclaimed…" Ibid., 311.

p. 92, "I experienced the greatest..." Ibid., 315.

p. 92, "While the first two movements…" Ibid., 315.

p. 94, "You really seem to be…" Ibid., 320.

p. 95, "You regard it only…" Susanna Reich, *Clara Schumann Piano Virtuoso* (New York: Clarion Books, 1999), 97.

p. 96, "What we have heard today…" Swafford, *Johannes Brahms,* 330.

CHAPTER SIX: From Sorrow to Symphony

p. 99, "I'll never write a symphony!" Swafford, *Johannes Brahms,* 334.

p. 100, "Why not make a new edition in a Minor key…" Ibid., 338.

p. 102, "It is long since I remember being moved…" Ibid., 351.

p. 105, "I'm in a really good mood today…" Ibid., 372.

p. 109, "from time to time I write highly useless pieces…" Ibid., 398.

CHAPTER SEVEN: Working Summers

p. 112, "That symphony is…" Swafford, *Johannes Brahms,* 444.

p. 112, "Unqualified Success." Ibid., 444.

p. 114, "I felt as if I were sitting on thorns…" Ibid., 459.

p. 116, "I can scarcely speak of it…" Ibid., 503.

p. 116, "Today we sing no more…" Ibid., 482.

p. 116, "No house, no homeland, no wife…" Ibid., 484.

p. 119, "Whoever has not heard Liszt…" Gal, *Johannes Brahms,* 33.

CHAPTER EIGHT: Farewell

p. 121, "I had wanted to extract…" Gal, *Johannes Brahms,* 89.

p. 122, "My whole life I've been…" Swafford, *Johannes Brahms,* 566.

p. 122, "Oh, if only we had clarinets…" Richard Carlin, *European Classical Music: 1600-1825* (New York: Facts on File Publications, 1988), 46.

p. 123, "Apart from Frau Schumann…one's children" Swafford, *Johannes Brahms,* 600.

p. 125, "…if you think the worst is expected…" Ibid., 607.

p. 126, "Will not our faces light up…" Gal, *Johannes Brahms,* 19.

Bibliography

Avins, Styra, ed. *Johannes Brahms: Life and Letters*. Oxford: Oxford University Press, 1997.

Bergamini, Andrea. *Beethoven and the Classical Age*. Hauppauge, NY: Barron's Educational Series, Inc., 1999.

Brook-Shepherd, Gordon. *The Austrians, A Thousand Year Odyssey*. New York: Carroll & Graf Publishers, Inc., 1996.

Brown, Jonathon. *Johannes Brahms: An Essential Guide to his Life and Works*. London: Pavilion Books Ltd., 1996.

Carlin, Richard. *European Classical Music: 1600-1825*. New York: Facts on File Publications, 1988.

Cavalletti, Carlo. *Chopin and the Romantic Age*. Hauppauge, NY: Barron's Educational Series, Inc., 2000.

Gal, Hans. *Johannes Brahms: His Work and Personality*. London: Weidenfeld and Nicolson, 1963.

Geiringer, Karl. *Brahms: His Life and Work*. New York: Da Capo, 1982.

Moore, Douglas. *From Madrigal to Modern Music*. New York: W.W. Norton & Company Inc., 1942.

Reich, Susanna. *Clara Schumann Piano Virtuoso*. New York: Clarion Books, 1999.

Sadie, Stanley. *The New Grove Dictionary of Music and Musicians*. Washington DC: Macmillan Publishers Limited, 1980.

Seroff, Victor. *Men Who Made Musical History*. New York: Funk & Wagnalls, 1969.

Swafford, Jan. *Johannes Brahms: A Biography*. New York: Alfred A. Knopf, 1997.

Ventura, Piero. *Great Composers*. New York: G.P. Putnam's Sons, 1988.

Wechsberg, Joseph. *The Pantheon Story of Music for Young People*. New York: Pantheon Books, 1968.

Web sites:

Humanities Web
www.humanitiesweb.org
A well-organized source of information on music from the Medieval period through the present. Also covers literature, visual arts, and history.

Johannes Brahms WebSource
www.johannesbrahms.org
Offers a biography, timelines, and useful Brahms-related links.

The Internet Public Library's Music History 102
www.ipl.org/div/mushist
A guide to Western composers and their music from the Middle Ages to the present.

Index